BEATLEOLOGY

A Magical Mystery Tour to Discover Your Inner Beatle

Adam Jaquette and Roger Jaquette

Aadamsmedia

Avon, Massachusetts

Published by
Adams Media, a division of F+W Media, Inc.
57 Littlefield Street, Avon, MA 02322. U.S.A.
www.adamsmedia.com

ISBN 10: 1-60550-064-X
ISBN 13: 978-1-60550-064-5

Printed in the United States of America.

J I H G F E D C B A

Library of Congress Cataloging-in-Publication Data
is available from the publisher.

This publication is designed to provide accurate and authoritative information with
regard to the subject matter covered. It is sold with the understanding that the publisher
is not engaged in rendering legal, accounting, or other professional advice. If legal advice
or other expert assistance is required, the services of a competent professional person
should be sought.

  —From a *Declaration of Principles* jointly adopted by a Committee of the
American Bar Association and a Committee of Publishers and Associations

Many of the designations used by manufacturers and sellers to distinguish their product
are claimed as trademarks. Where those designations appear in this book and Adams
Media was aware of a trademark claim, the designations have been printed with initial
capital letters.

Illustration p.13 © 2009 Jupiterimages
Record Image © Simfo

*This book is available at quantity discounts for bulk purchases.
For information, please call 1-800-289-0963.*

TABLE OF
CONTENTS

To Bill (George),
Leslee (Ringo),
and Phyllis (Ringo).

Chapter 1

MEET THE BEATLES

Congratulations. You have just taken the first step in the next phase of human evolution: Beatleology. Throughout human existence, we have sought to explain the human condition through various means. Religion, science, and philosophy have all been humanity's futile attempts to understand the world around it. Finally, our quest is over.

What Is Beatleology?

Do you relate to one of the Beatles more than the others? Are you serious and intense like John Lennon? Or are you more at ease with the world like Ringo? Maybe you're quiet and thoughtful like George Harrison? Or perhaps you're sweet and embracing like Paul McCartney. If so, there is a good reason.

For centuries, psychology has searched for a unifying theory of human personality that has finally led to its logical conclusion: the Beatles. Through exhaustive research, we have found that all human actions, interactions, and relationships are governed by the laws of Beatleology. Every aspect of your existence—be it your love life, career, or family life—is defined by your "Inner Beatle." Beatleology is the belief that every conceivable personality type can be classified as one of the four Beatles: John, Paul, George, or Ringo. To put it simply, each one of us "is" a Beatle.

Each of us has an Inner Beatle. Your mom was a Beatle. So was your dad. And which Beatle they were defined their relationship. You may have inherited one of their Beatles, or were given your own, which in turn defines all of your future relationships with your fellow human beings (all of whom each have their own Inner Beatle). Beatleology allows you to discover your Inner Beatle and those of your friends and loved ones. It helps you understand who are the best matches for your Inner Beatle and which people are the worst fits. Beatleology uses the iconic personalities of the Fab Four to help you identify who you are as an individual and with whom you work best in love and life. At its essence, Beatleology is a method for understanding yourself and those around you.

The aim of this book is to help you identify your true Inner Beatle and to teach you how to use Beatleology to understand the complex dynamics of all your relationships.

Beatleology: The Steps

To achieve a greater understanding of your Inner Beatle and those of your fellow humans, it is critical to follow the steps of Beatleology. Just as a child cannot learn to run before he learns to walk, you cannot fully appreciate others' Inner Beatles without first understanding your own. Therefore, the first step is to correctly identify your Inner Beatle. Second, the Beatleologist must learn to embrace his or her Inner Beatle. Even if you wanted to be a Paul because he was so darn cute, but you turned out to be Ringo, do not be discouraged. All Beatle Signs are created equal. The next step in Beatleology involves identifying the Inner Beatles of your family, friends, and coworkers in order to create a sense of harmony in your life. Finally, the Beatleologist must learn to live with all our fellow Beatles.

Step 1: Identify Your Inner Beatle

Your Inner Beatle is your personality type, your astrological sign, your totem, and your destiny all rolled into one. You do not choose your Inner Beatle. You simply *are* your Inner Beatle. For some of us, it's easy to identify our Beatle personality. For others, it's not so clear. For example, with his outgoing personality, can-do attitude, and positive outlook (not to mention his love of strong women), former president Bill Clinton is obviously a Paul. However, a president like Gerald Ford was not as obvious. Surprisingly, he was *also* a Paul. Gerald Ford possessed a down-to-earth charm. He attempted to unify the country and embraced trendy causes like Puerto Rican statehood.

Obviously, not all Johns, Pauls, Georges, and Ringos have the exact same personality traits. Race, nationality, education, and experience all affect how our Beatle Sign manifests itself. For instance, a traditional Japanese Ringo is very different from a Ringo who lives in the Castro district of San Francisco and works as an interior designer. However, they do share a similar worldview that reveals itself within the context of who they are. Also, not every John will exhibit all of the traits of a typical John. This is partly due to the fact that many people have Minor Beatle Signs. There will be more on this topic later, but simply put, minor signs represent your recessive personality traits, those which only shine through under certain circumstances.

- When trying to identify your Beatle Sign, it's important to look at your overall personality.
- To identify your Inner Beatle, use the Beatleology Quiz in Chapter 2 and descriptions of each Beatle personality. It should become clear to you which Beatle you in fact "are." Identifying your true Inner Beatle is the first step to personal enlightenment.

Step 2: Embrace Your Beatle

- The second step involves using your newfound knowledge of your Inner Beatle's intricacies, strengths, weaknesses, and quirks to live a more fulfilling life. Simply knowing your Inner Beatle is not enough. You must act in accordance with your Inner Beatle to achieve your full potential.
- Be proud to be your Beatle Sign, knowing that all signs have their own place in the Beatle-verse. One sign does not have more value

than another. A John trying to be a Ringo is like a Buddhist monk trying to be a reggae singer; he can try, but it simply isn't in him. Take comfort in the fact that as a particular Beatle Sign, there are some things you are going to do well and certain things you are not. For example, Ringos make great car salespeople, politicians, and Baptist ministers, but lousy chemists, cartographers, or Russian Orthodox priests. Georges make great patent attorneys, engineers, and yoga instructors but lousy telemarketers, commodity traders, or aerobics instructors. The world needs all of these to go around (except tele-marketers). In the harmony and beauty of the natural order, there is a Beatle Sign for everything.

Step 3: Identify Your Fellow Beatles

- Once you have begun to live in harmony with your Beatle Sign, it is important to identify the Inner Beatle of the people in your life. Only by knowing your family members', coworkers', and friends' Beatle Signs, can you ever truly hope to understand them and the dynamics of your relationship.

Step 4: Live Harmoniously with Other Beatle Signs

Only when you have mastered yourself, can you master your sur-roundings. The fourth step in Beatleology involves using your wisdom to coexist with all other Beatles and to improve your relationships. By knowing your boss's Inner Beatle, you can forge a more productive relationship with him. For instance, being aware that your boss is a Paul will help you understand why he must organize copious team-building events and give employee evaluations four times a year.

We all have to live with other Beatles. Not all Beatles get along in all of our various relationships. For example, Paris Hilton's Ringo and Nicole Richie's Ringo can have a lot of fun, but will sometimes add up to too much Ringo. Whereas, if Paris Hilton teamed up with Noam Chomsky's George, they may not have as much fun, but they might actually accomplish something. There are other pairings that work well and those that don't. For example, two Pauls can work great in love. But two Johns will end in fights, bitter name-calling, and possible legal action. Beatle relationships are intricate with no two being exactly alike.

Overview of Beatle Personalities

The following are brief overviews of the four Beatles signs. Much more will be found in the John, Paul, George, and Ringo chapters.

Where do you fit in?

John: The Smart One

John Lennon, the most iconic of the group, lived a life full of extremes. Individuals who are Johns share this tendency. Johns can be brilliant and charming but can also be full of anger and short-sightedness. Many Johns are marked by a proverbial chip-on-the-shoulder attitude toward life. People of this sign feel as if they have something to prove and often act accordingly. This can manifest itself as a strong, intense personality. This is not to say that Johns can't be fun. In fact, they are frequently hilarious and amusing but with an edge. Johns often exhibit melancholy and tend to see the world in terms of black-and-white absolutes. They are always thinking and evaluating existence, but this contemplation rarely leads to a peaceful soul. Johns see human existence as hierarchical and class-driven.

They want to fight the system but also claw to be top dog within it. The young John Lennon was constantly fighting at school to achieve social status. Later in life, with their famous "Bed-Ins," John and Yoko fought in a similarly absurd fashion, but this time for peace in Vietnam. Johns are the classic "rebels with a cause," but that cause is frequently themselves. They have a tendency to be:

- Intelligent
- Brooding
- Showoffy
- Bipolar
- Able to hold a grudge
- Melancholy
- Loyal
- Flippant
- Creative
- Dominating
- Instigating
- Scheming
- Insane
- Corruptible
- Stressed

Paul: The Cute One

In contrast to John, there is Paul. Pauls tend to be optimistic and see challenges as opportunities and embrace what's good in life. They also have a driven, perfectionist side to their personality, which can make them hard to deal with. Many Pauls have dominating personalities that often take over a room. They are outgoing and gregarious which often makes them well liked. Pauls have a healthy ego and self-love that can sometimes run amok. Pauls also have romanticized notions of love and relationships. The "don't look back" fast-paced optimism of a Paul is often incompatible with the more thoughtful, cautious George sign. Pauls never give up, but they also don't know when to quit. Other Beatle Signs may find Pauls annoying for aggressiveness and a tendency to have an idealistic view of the world around them. Pauls have a tendency to be:

- Enthusiastic
- Positive
- Energetic
- Cutesy
- Corny
- Sentimental

- Perfectionist
- Overbearing
- Power-hungry
- Screwed in divorce
- Trendy
- Popular

George: The Shy One

Like Johns, Georges tend to be thoughtful, contemplative individuals. Unlike Johns, Georges tend to be more reserved and often have a measure of inner peace that Johns lack. Many Georges are introverted or shy in certain situations, but they can be quite amiable when they are within their comfort zone. Georges are realistic and pragmatic, knowing that there is both good and bad in all things. Unlike Johns, Georges tend to accept life for what it is. Georges can be passive-aggressive and prefer to work behind the scenes rather than in front. They are highly individualistic which is why they hate team-building exercises and group projects. Many Georges would just rather do all the work themselves. They often clash with Pauls because they resent Paul's tendency to be an overbearing, pushy perfectionist. Georges have a tendency to be:

- Shy
- Spiritual
- Fastidious
- Quiet
- Reserved
- Intellectual
- Brooding
- Secretive
- Passive-aggressive
- Withdrawn
- Covetous

Ringo: The Funny One

Everybody loves a Ringo. Ringos have an easygoing charisma and charm. Other signs enjoy Ringos because they are often disarming. You can relax when hanging around a Ringo because they don't have to be center stage. Ringos make welcoming and inclusive individuals, which partly accounts for their general popularity. A Ringo's creativity manifests itself as a collaborative effort rather than as a Paul's one-man band. Sometimes Ringos are seen as all charm and no substance, but this is usually a misconception. Ringos not only work well with all other Beatle Signs, but they also do well with other Ringos (a unique quality of all the Beatle Signs). For the most part Ringos take life in stride and are well-adjusted individuals. Ringos have a tendency to be:

- Funny
- Charming
- Lighthearted
- Underappreciated
- Friendly
- Forgiving
- Flexible
- Content
- Hedonistic
- Lazy
- Fraternal

All Inner Beatles Are Created Equally

Without one of their members, the Beatles would still be playing five gigs a day in Hamburg to drunken Germans for wiener schnitzel and beer. Their success can only be attributed to the combination of the four individuals. Without Paul, they would have lost one of their strongest songwriters. Without Ringo, they would have lost some of their playful attitude. Without John, they would have lost their experimental side. Without George, they would have lacked some fine musicianship and songwriting. Therefore, all Beatle Signs truly are created equal.

John and Paul are the most iconic of the Beatles and are often misconceived as the most important members of the band. They are also sometimes mistakenly thought of as the most desirable Beatle Signs. Embrace whatever Beatle Sign you are. Georges and Ringos should be just as proud as Pauls or Johns.

Now, armed with your new, life-altering understanding of Beatleology, it's time to discover your Beatle Sign. Take the "I Am the Walrus" quiz in Chapter 2. You might be surprised. You might not be who you expected.

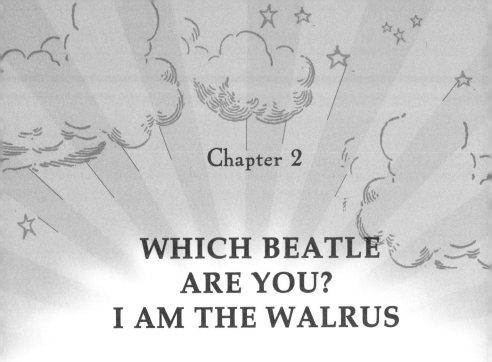

Chapter 2

WHICH BEATLE ARE YOU? I AM THE WALRUS

Which Beatle are you? It's not always an easy question to answer. Your Inner Beatle controls not only your relationships, habits, and behaviors but also part of your destiny. It's critical to know precisely which Beatle you are. Being in touch with your Beatle Sign is integral for any type of meaningful personal development.

Some Inner Beatles are obvious. Former president Ronald Reagan was obviously a Ringo. Beethoven was clearly a John; whereas, Gandhi had an Inner Paul. Tom Wolfe is classic George. (Now, that's a Fab Four.) Many of you probably have a clear idea of your Inner Beatle already.

However, for some of us, discovering our Inner Beatle is not always so intuitive. Often, the way in which we view ourselves is radically different than how others do. Therefore, it's necessary to get an unbiased answer to the profound question, "Which Beatle am I?" With this simple, multiple-choice quiz, your Beatle Sign will reveal itself. This powerful epiphany may bring a new understanding of yourself and the world around you.

There's good news and bad news. First, the good news: This isn't the SAT. The bad news is you still have to be 100 percent honest (at least with yourself).

The following questions are designed to help you identify your Inner Beatle. It is important to answer as truthfully and honestly as possible. Self-deception will only result in a "false Beatle," which can have deep ramifications in the future. Avoid the temptation to answer the questions with a result in mind. You many want to be a John because you enjoy his music or think highly of him, but cosmically your Beatle Sign is something else. It's important to be open to any outcome. After all, the Beatle-verse is a cosmic quartet.

Do not fret if you don't answer each question as your Inner Beatle. Individuals are complex and may not share every single trait of their Beatle Sign. Besides, you might have a minor sign. Look at the overall results and score at the end of the quiz to determine your Inner Beatle.

Lastly, remember that some of the questions are theoretical. Think of which answer matches you metaphorically, not just literally. Some questions are an extrapolation of your personality to a more severe degree.

Good luck.

The Quiz

Which Beatle Are You?

Part I: Work

1. In my career, my feelings regarding success are _____.

Ⓐ I feel I must succeed at any cost and am willing to do anything to achieve it. Ⓑ As long as the check doesn't bounce, I'm cool. To me, work is just one aspect of life. Ⓒ I would like to succeed but am not willing to sell my soul for it. Ⓓ I feel I deserve success and will be successful in any endeavor.

2. I see my boss as_____.

Ⓐ Someone to work with and help me as long as he or she is not too domineering. Ⓑ Someone to look up to. I like my boss and strive to be in his or her position. Ⓒ Just another bloke. Bosses are a fact of life. Ⓓ A bourgeois capitalist pig who will be the first one against the wall when the revolution comes. They will keep me down unless they respect my autonomy.

3. In my relationships with my coworkers, I feel _____.

Ⓐ They are important as a support for me and my work (as long as they do as I say). Ⓑ They can help me polish an idea or project but can also drag down my work. Ⓒ They are just another bunch of blokes. I enjoy my coworkers if they are not overly serious or stressful. Ⓓ I like my coworkers as long as they don't try to dominate the workplace.

4. When picking a career, I look for _____.

Ⓐ Independence and a laidback atmosphere. Ⓑ Stability in a company, financial gain, and a friendly environment. Ⓒ A dynamic work environment with lots of opportunity for advancement. Ⓓ A job that allows me a certain degree of freedom, autonomy, and the ability to express myself.

5. During my lunch hour, I _____.

Ⓐ Am out at a restaurant having nachos and a beer. Ⓑ Am working on my personal projects like art, music, and writing. Ⓒ Am using the time to pick up my dry cleaning or working ahead. Ⓓ Am the center of the conversation in the lunchroom.

6. I arrive at work _____.

Ⓐ Early, but leave early. Ⓑ Early and stay late. Ⓒ Late, but stay late. Ⓓ Whenever I arrive *is* on time.

7. Things I have stolen from work include _____.

Ⓐ My coworker's client list but not physical items. Ⓑ Laptops, light bulbs, copper wire from the wall, anything that's not bolted down. Ⓒ Drinks on the expense report and paper clips. Ⓓ Only big items I know I can get away with.

8. My obligation toward work is _____.

Ⓐ I need my job for money, but my real obligation is to myself. Ⓑ I want to have the reputation as doing my best, but deep down I don't care. Ⓒ I feel obligated to do my best and succeed. Ⓓ I do my work so I deserve to get paid.

9. When I quit a job, I _____.

Ⓐ Leave well liked and on good terms. Ⓑ Send around a goodbye e-mail thanking everyone. Ⓒ Burn my bridges and tell everyone to piss off. Ⓓ Quietly walk away, but fantasize about burning the place down.

10. When I go on vacation, _____.

Ⓐ I check in occasionally, but prefer not to. Ⓑ I never check my messages or e-mail. Whatever it is can wait. Ⓒ I try not to check in but can't help thinking about work. Ⓓ I am in constant contact and check messages daily.

Part II: Relationships

1. In a lover or a spouse, I look for _____.

Ⓐ Someone who supports and adores me. Ⓑ A true partner, someone who challenges me. Ⓒ A loving, easygoing partner. Ⓓ Fun, love, and sex.

2. Dating is _____.

Ⓐ A fun way to meet people and possibly get some action. Ⓑ A pain in the neck. Ⓒ An opportunity for me to be charming and adored. Ⓓ A huge waste of time. We should cut right to a stiflingly codependent relationship.

3. In a long-term relationship, I tend to be _____.

Ⓐ Codependent at the expense of my other relationships. Ⓑ Stable and avoid relationship drama. Ⓒ Committed but not overly analytical about my feelings. Ⓓ The dominant partner and the center of attention. We do what I want.

4. After a breakup, I _____.

Ⓐ Am also hurt and have a period of quiet reflection. Ⓑ Am hurt (especially my ego) and wonder why someone would give me up. Ⓒ Am emotionally crushed and often drunkenly call my ex. Ⓓ Realize it wasn't meant to be and recover quickly.

5. During sex, I am _____.

Ⓐ A top. Ⓑ A bottom. Ⓒ A top, bottom, or side. Ⓓ Tied to the bedpost.

6. On a first date, _____.

Ⓐ I find myself in Vegas getting married by Elvis. I quickly think he or she is "the one." Ⓑ I read him or her some of my poetry, and I am very open about my feelings. I, too, quickly think he or she is "the one." Ⓒ I just want to go out and have a good time. Ⓓ I try to be myself but have trouble showing my true personality.

7. When I propose marriage, _____.

Ⓐ It's going to be a grand gesture such as on the Dodgers' scoreboard or while we're sky-diving. Ⓑ It will be because we can't stand it anymore and must be together. My proposal will be hopelessly romantic and memorable. Ⓒ It's either because I knocked her up or am on hard drugs. Ⓓ I have thought about the ramifications and realize I truly want it.

8. I view sex as _____.

Ⓐ A way to express myself and the spiritual union with my partner. Ⓑ An intimate expression of love and a way to get me rocks off. Ⓒ A way to achieve love and affirmation. Ⓓ A fun way to relax and feel good.

9. My thoughts on infidelity are —————.

Ⓐ I'm not willing to cheat because I don't want to be viewed as that sort of person. Ⓑ It's easier to be monogamous than cheat on my lover. I like to keep my love life simple. Ⓒ If I believe in the relationship, I will be monogamous. But if I don't truly care, I'm willing to cheat. Ⓓ If it feels good, do it.

10. Complete this sentence: I hate —————.

Ⓐ War, strong women. Ⓑ Ex-girlfriends, new girlfriends. Ⓒ Egomaniacal jerks, deep breathing. Ⓓ Myself, myself.

Part III: Family

1. When it comes to raising children, —————.

Ⓐ I can be a terrible or amazing parent. If the circumstances are right, I will be a dedicated and loving mom or dad but if I'm forced into parenthood, I can also be distant. Ⓑ Kids are a fun, important aspect of my life. They should not, however, interfere too much with my marriage and other pursuits. Ⓒ I will love my kids, if I choose to have them. I am likely to see my children as friends when they grow a little older. Ⓓ I just love kids and am a dedicated mother or father.

2. Family is important to me because —————.

Ⓐ They bring me joy. Ⓑ They are friends and people who share my interests and beliefs. Ⓒ I love my family deeply and they support me. Ⓓ They are the only people I can trust and count on in life.

3. Which describes your role in your family? _____

Ⓐ I am just one member of the family. We share decisions and responsibilities. Ⓑ I'm head of the family. I often plan activities, vacations, and family rules. Ⓒ I'm just here for the beer. I'm happy to let others worry about the Thanksgiving centerpiece or yell at the kids for not washing their hands. Ⓓ Deep down I feel I'm the head of the family, but if people want to take initiative, that's fine by me.

4. When I was growing up, my mother and father were _____.

Ⓐ Supportive and loving. I got very lucky. Ⓑ Worried about me. We didn't always get along. Ⓒ Very giving. They gave me a great deal of freedom. Ⓓ They weren't perfect, but my parents did the best they could and I don't blame them for much.

5. An ideal family vacation is _____.

Ⓐ A romantic get-away with just me and the old lady (or man). Ⓑ Lying on a beach in the Caribbean. Ⓒ Traveling all together, possibly in an RV or boat. Ⓓ Seeing nature or culturally significant places.

Part IV: Morality

1. Do I owe a debt to society? _____

Ⓐ Anyone as talented and brilliant as me owes a debt to society. Ⓑ I'm lucky to be literate, fed, and employed. Life could be a lot worse. Ⓒ I don't owe the world anything. Life is inherently unfair. Ⓓ I didn't know I borrowed any money. Honestly, I don't give it a great deal of thought. In the words of that famous philosopher, "I am what I am."

2. Is stealing ever justifiable? _____

Ⓐ Stealing is wrong. It hurts others. Ⓑ I wouldn't steal; I'd just ask for it if I could. Stealing is a last resort. Ⓒ Stealing isn't 100 percent wrong. If you have to steal formula for a hungry baby, that doesn't make you a bad person. Ⓓ Sure. I nick things all the time. Wal-Mart isn't going to miss a few Xbox games.

3. You've arrested a *suspected* terrorist. He may be aware of when and where a terrorist attack will occur but will only reveal the truth through painful torture. Would you torture him? _____

Ⓐ If he's only a suspected terrorist, he might also just be an innocent person. How can I be sure he really knows something about an imminent attack? I'm just not 100 percent sure. Ⓑ Yes. First of all, he's a terrorist and deserves to be tortured. Second, by torturing him, I will get information that can save lives. Not doing so would mean the death of others. Ⓒ Yes. It might secretly be enjoyable. Ⓓ Couldn't somebody else, like Jack Bauer, do this?

4. Is there such a thing as right and wrong? _____

Ⓐ Who knows? These ethical questions are annoyingly pretentious. Ⓑ I'm not sure. I believe in right and wrong, but I'm not sure they are absolutes. Ⓒ They are subjective. Time, culture, and experience play an important role in determining these ideas. Ⓓ There is an objective right and wrong. For instance, it is wrong to commit murder or rape.

5. Is it ever acceptable to lie? _____

Ⓐ Since I often speak off the cuff, I rarely tell little white lies. Ⓑ I try not to lie, but sometimes it's unavoidable. Little white lies are okay. Ⓒ I lie all the time. Lying can save other people's feelings and my butt. Ⓓ Omission isn't technically lying. I'll lie to save people's feelings and cover my ass at work.

Part V: Religion and Spirituality

1. Do you believe in God? _____

Ⓐ I believe in God and am confident He exists. Ⓑ If there is a God, He (or She) is more of a higher power or a set of moral truths. Ⓒ I'm not honestly sure. Part of me hopes there is a God, but I'm not positive. Ⓓ There is no God: Religion is just opium for the masses.

2. What is God like? _____

Ⓐ God is whatever you want him to be. Ⓑ God is very much human. He is imperfect but also has positive traits such as humor. Ⓒ God is more of a force or idea. I don't see God as a literal person. Ⓓ I see God as a stoic person who created us in His own image. He is upset when we sin.

3. Complete this sentence: I _____
spiritual _____ religious.

Ⓐ Am spiritual but not religious. Ⓑ Am both spiritual and religious. Ⓒ Am somewhat spiritual and somewhat religious. Ⓓ Am neither spiritual nor religious.

4. As a kid, I saw church as _____.

Ⓐ An annoying waste of time my parents dragged me to. Ⓑ I made it fun, whether through friends or having my own good time. Ⓒ A fun time. I have many positive memories of church. Ⓓ A mixed memory. I enjoyed the social aspect of church but couldn't buy into all of its rules and rituals.

5. Do pets go to heaven? _____

Ⓐ If there is a heaven, absolutely. Ⓑ Yes or they are reborn. Ⓒ No, animals don't have souls like humans. Ⓓ Little Fluffy might not get into heaven?

Part VI: Money

1. How are you with money? _____

Ⓐ I'm very good with money. I am rarely broke. Ⓑ I'm pretty good with money, but I can also justify unnecessary purchases. Ⓒ I'm good with money, but there are times it just seems to fly out of my pocket. Ⓓ I like to spend money and sometimes it gets me into trouble.

2. At the end of the month, _____.

Ⓐ There's a good chance I'll come out a bit short. Ⓑ I can tell you how much I will have left almost to the penny. Ⓒ I don't keep track of my finances too closely, but I know that I will come out ahead most months. Ⓓ I'm okay because I tend to have a nice reserve.

3. What do you spend on your vacations? _____

Ⓐ I like to relax and feel very comfortable on my vacations. I travel in style, which doesn't come cheap. Ⓑ Since I live frugally, I can afford most reasonable vacations. Ⓒ I tend to spend a bit too much on my holidays, but I am willing to stay in a cheap motel if it gets me where I want to be. Ⓓ Señor Frog's has my photo up behind the bar.

4. If I won the lottery, I would —————.

> **A** Never work my crappy job again. See ya, suckers! **B** Use the money to make myself financially secure even if it meant not changing my lifestyle for the better. **C** Enjoy some of the money. I deserve a really nice car and house. **D** PAR-TY!

5. How much did you spend on your last car? —————

> **A** It's just a car. I got the best I could afford. **B** I love nice things so I bought a nice car. It might have been a bit out of my budget. **C** I bought an inexpensive, yet environmentally friendly car. **D** I budgeted for my car and am happy with my purchase.

Part VII: Miscellaneous

1. What kind of setting makes you the most comfortable? —————

> **A** A group of friends and other people who think I am clever. In work, I prefer to go it alone or with a partner. **B** Large gatherings and parties. In work, I prefer places with a certain amount of regimentation. **C** I try to avoid party settings and prefer intimate gatherings. In work, I prefer to work alone. **D** Parties are good, but so are small groups. At work, I enjoy being part of a team, especially if they appreciate me.

2. Who do you turn to in time of need? —————

> **A** Only a couple of very trusted people. I don't trust everyone with all of the details of my life. I often compartmentalize people for different things. **B** I turn to my very trusted friends. I don't feel they will judge me. **C** No one at all. Maybe a trusted mother figure. **D** Everyone. Friends, parents, coworkers.

3. What genre of books do you enjoy? _____

Ⓐ Romance novels, photography books, young adult novels. I'm not a huge reader. Ⓑ Fiction and nonfiction on topics that interest me. Ⓒ Nonfiction, spirituality. I enjoy reading about people and the human condition. Ⓓ Mysteries, thrillers, science fiction, and anything that is enjoyable. I don't read books to make myself look cool.

4. How politically aware are you? _____

Ⓐ I like candidates like Dennis Kucinich or Ron Paul (depending on political tastes). Politically, I focus more on causes like the environment, abortion, and war. Ⓑ I'm not overly political. I'm aware of major candidates and elections but might have a hard time quoting policy. Ⓒ Sometimes I vote, sometimes I forget. I'm more interested in local politics. Ⓓ I have a strong interest in politics but have a pragmatic attitude toward candidates. There's just no way a half-literate actor could become president (oh, wait).

5. If you were to commit suicide, _____.

Ⓐ I would never commit suicide. I just couldn't do it. Ⓑ I would have to do it in a painless way. Ⓒ I'd only do it to save my children or if I were terminally ill. Ⓓ I'd take everyone with me first.

Results

Now comes the exciting part. Which Beatle are you? Use the scoring guide in the Appendix to determine your Inner Beatle. You may be surprised at the results, or you might already have a good inkling of your Beatle Sign. Either way, the results of this test can help individuals realize who they truly are.

Good luck!

What If My Results Don't Match My Gut Feeling?

Maybe you took the test, started to read the Beatle Sign descriptions, and lo and behold, you don't think your test results are accurate. What do you do? Which Beatle are you truly?

Remember, the Inner Beatle quiz is only one tool that can be used to identify your Beatle Sign. Like your parents told you about your SAT scores, it's only one test. It doesn't necessarily define who you are. If you feel strongly that you are a different sign, then it's probably true. To help you be more objective, have friends and loved ones read that description to see if they agree that it matches. Sometimes we perceive ourselves in a radically different light than others do.

Beatleology is not an exact science. Use all of the tools available to you to determine your Beatle Sign.

Why Everybody Thinks They Are a John (but Very Few People Are)

Despite what a lot of people want to believe, not everyone is a John. In fact, Johns are the least prevalent sign in Beatleology. By far there are many more Georges, Ringos, and especially Pauls in the world today. So, why does everyone want to believe they are a John, you ask? Simply put, most tend to view John Lennon as the soul behind the Beatles. They see him as the most artistic, most intelligent, and most challenging of the Fab Four (let's face it, "Hey Jude" isn't exactly Tolstoy). Therefore, in the world of the Beatles, John is often assigned more value. Additionally, since his murder and martyrdom, John has been idealized and elevated to a deity-like status (apparently they forgot about the Plastic Ono Band). Thanks to Wings and Paul's attempts at composing symphonies, we all see he is human, but John is now a mythological figure.

So, needless to say, everyone wants to be a John because of the myth. While John is arguably one of the most important Beatles in terms of his contributions to the music, in strict Beatleology, a John sign has no more value than a Ringo.

Chapter 3

INNER JOHN: REVOLUTION

Are you or someone you love a mad genius? A troubled artist? Ahead of your time? Gifted? Talented? Full of melancholy and quiet charm? Do you feel you're the smartest one in the room and yet you don't want to be the center of attention? Is your life full of tragedy and yet you persevere? Do you make terrible choices when it comes to relationships?

Does your spouse or lover bring out the worst in you? Did you have a promising career as a dental hygienist before your boyfriend got you addicted to meth? If you answered "yes" to many of these questions, there is a good chance you are a John. Johns are often the easiest sign to spot, but the least understood.

IDENTIFYING A JOHN: A QUICK CHECK

Are you a John? Find out if the following examples describe you or a loved one.

- ☐ You are often troubled by ideas or problems that others can seemingly shrug off.
- ☐ You can hold resentments or grudges for a long time.
- ☐ You have a hard time relaxing and/or sleeping.
- ☐ Social justice is important to you. You feel the world is inherently unfair.
- ☐ You have trouble taking criticism.
- ☐ In romance, you pick partners who are equals and challenge you intellectually.
- ☐ You are almost always busy with work or personal projects to fulfill your creative needs. You don't understand people who are bored (like that guy who wins the lottery and keeps his day job).
- ☐ You tend to see the world pessimistically, yet hope for the best.
- ☐ You hope to make a good impression and have people think well of you.
- ☐ You have a dark, edgy sense of humor that might offend more sensitive people.

- [ ] You think you're a genius and the rest of the world is full of fools.
- [ ] You hate stupid trends like Lance Armstrong bracelets, Dr. Phil, and reality TV.
- [ ] You can also make poor decisions in your love life (Yoko Ono, that girl who got you involved in a bar fight with the Chicago Bears' defensive line, etc.).
- [ ] You are a dedicated and loving parent or pet owner (however, you refuse to buy your dog a $350 cashmere sweater—see Inner Paul).
- [ ] You have a strong work ethic, yet secretly hope your office gets destroyed by Godzilla.

What Does It Mean to Be a John?

Simply put, Johns are people of extremes. One minute Johns may be overly serious and intense. The next, they may seem light and flippant. With a John, you are never sure who you are going to get. Johns are deep, contemplative thinkers with a strong bent toward the arts or pushing the boundaries of their careers. They tend to take life seriously, but hide the fact behind humor. They can be moody and withdrawn, and yet are often extremely engaging and fascinating people. Frequently, Johns exhibit feelings of superiority, being the superman in a world of fools. In the work place, Johns are often very helpful to have around, ensuring the work you don't want to do gets done. If anyone is going to cure world hunger, it's going to be a John. If anyone is going to write three hundred haiku poems about his girlfriend, it's a John. And frankly, we need people who are going to take a year of their life and move to Botswana to help fight AIDS.

Positive Characteristics

Creative

Intelligent

Charming

Hardworking

Contemplative

Productive

Loyal

On a personal level, Johns can be quite touching and sensitive people. While they often have a great deal of empathy, they can come off as cold and sometimes bitter individuals.

Johns are frequently the most troubled sign in Beatleology, partly because Johns overdramatize everything and partly because they are attracted to people who bring out their worst qualities, causing their downfall (see Chaper 8). Despite their acute creative side, Johns have a tendency to think everything they do is wonderful, brilliant, and misunderstood. It's often important for Johns to have a trustworthy censor to help them find the diamond in the rough, just as the real John Lennon had a foil in Paul McCartney.

As seen in the relationship between John Lennon and Yoko Ono, Johns have the tendency to make bad relationship decisions. To put it not-so-nicely, despite their intelligence and creativity, Johns, for whatever reason, are attracted to sluts, rednecks, losers, deadbeats, hangers-on, drug addicts, or anyone who might screw up their lives. No one knows why the most powerful sign in Beatleology is drawn to such destructive forces. It is one of the great dichotomies of the Beatleverse.

Inversely, Johns are, on occasion, attracted to people who act as a very positive influence on their lives (like Cynthia Lennon). These people tend to steer Johns away from their destructive behaviors. Unfortunately, most Johns quickly grow bored with these partners. Johns should be aware of their tendency to be attracted to the wrong sort of person, and pick partners who are more similar to a Cynthia than a Yoko.

Johns are predisposed to madness and anger. Their indignation and insanity is part and parcel of their creative genius. After all, a person can't have a unique worldview without being a little unique. But a great deal of their tendency toward psychosis is due to the fact that Johns can't stand being in a world populated with utter fools. Johns, for some reason, feel offended by the mere existence of stupid people and the idiocy that has marked modern life.

 Negative Characteristics

Impulsive
Poor decision-maker
Condescending
Distant
Conceited
Insensitive
Narcissistic
Corruptible
Reactionary
Angry
Dominating
Tendency toward insanity

John Lennon's Life

John Lennon's life was filled with music, genius, excess, reclusiveness, and tragedy. Many elements went into making the man that was John Lennon. He was a complex, often misunderstood figure—just like most Johns in Beatleology.

Like many Johns, John Lennon's life at an early age shaped who he became. Much of the proverbial chip on his shoulder and urgency to succeed stems from the early tragedies that marked his youth. This is true of many Johns who often go through life as if they have something to prove, a sense that they must light the world on fire.

John Winston Ono Lennon was born on October 9, 1940, in Liverpool, England, to Julia and Alfred "Freddie" Lennon. John was born during a German air raid, an appropriate symbol of the tumultuous life to come. At the time, Alfred was away at sea as a merchant marine. Soon after his son's birth, Alfred went AWOL from his job and Julia stopped receiving his much-needed income. Throughout the remainder of his life, John was troubled by his father's departure.

John's childhood went from bad to worse. After his father skipped out on the family, Julia would go on to have a daughter, Victoria, with another man. Julia was so ashamed of John's half-sister that she was quickly given up for adoption. Throughout the rest of his life, John would never know his lost sister. After giving Victoria up for adoption, Julia then proceeded to move into a small flat with a new boyfriend, John Dykins. Social services were soon called based on a report that the unwed couple and young John were sleeping in the same bed. John was quickly placed with his aunt Mimi and her husband George, a middle-class couple from Liverpool who had no children of their own.

The remainder of John's childhood and adolescence went comparatively smoothly. But as one can see, those early childhood experiences left a sense of bitter resentment, which partly drove Lennon to become a musical visionary. It was with Mimi and George that John was exposed to the more creative, inquisitive side of life. Mimi read short stories with her nephew and George encouraged him with the harmonica.

John did not lose all contact with his mother. In fact, he often went over to her house to play the banjo and piano. But more important, it was at his mother's house that he heard his first Elvis Presley records. She encouraged his desire to play the guitar, while Aunt Mimi hoped he would one day grow out of it.

After passing a difficult exam, John was admitted to the Quarry Bank Grammar School at the age of twelve where he met future Beatle Paul McCartney. Along with Stuart Sutcliffe and a young George Harrison, John and Paul started the Quarrymen, in reference to their school. At first they played a short-lived subgenre of rock-and-roll known as skiffle. The band quickly found it limiting and changed to more straightforward, blues-based rock music.

Just as John's star was about to rise, tragedy hit his life again. In 1958, John's mother was killed in a car accident by a drunken off-duty police officer. This incident brought John and Paul much closer together since Paul's mom had died of cancer two years earlier. Women would continue to play a very important role in both men's lives.

Throughout 1960 to 1962, the Beatles, pre-Ringo, played in small clubs in Hamburg, Germany, before being deported. In 1961, the band returned home to Liverpool where they began to garner a reputation as a good rock act. In 1962, former bassist and Lennon friend Stuart Sutcliffe died of a brain hemorrhage. Again, John found himself surrounded by the deaths of those closest to him.

After returning to Liverpool, John's girlfriend, Cynthia, became pregnant. The two were married in August 1962. Brian Epstein, the Beatles' manager, insisted that the marriage and the subsequent birth of Julian Lennon (named for John's mother, Julia) be kept a secret, but the secret was short-lived.

In 1962 the Beatles signed their first record contract. In October of that year, the Fab Four released their first single, "Love Me Do," cowritten by John and Paul. In the early years of the group, many songs were correctly credited to Lennon-McCartney. Their partnership created some of the greatest music of the twentieth century. However, like many of John's relationships, things quickly grew testy. Their working relationship was soon very strained with each man composing songs independently.

Throughout the remainder of the 1960s, the Beatles grew in popularity thanks to radio play and performances on *The Ed Sullivan Show*, which launched them into international superstardom. Worldwide Beatlemania quickly followed, changing John's life forever. The year 1968 marked the beginning of the end. John had been "experimenting" with LSD for some time, which only added to his more erratic tendencies and instability. He soon met and fell in love with Japanese conceptual artist Yoko Ono. Later that year he and Cynthia were divorced.

In 1969 John Lennon announced he was leaving the Beatles and started a solo career with the powerful backing of Yoko Ono, whose musical ability was only matched by that of Linda McCartney. From 1970 to 1975, John wrote and recorded some memorable and not-so-memorable music including "Imagine" and "Fame," which he wrote for David Bowie.

In 1975, with the birth of his second son, Sean Lennon, John decided to retire from the music industry. For the next five years,

John raised his second son and happily played the role of house husband. Then, in 1980, John and Yoko began recording tracks for the *Double Fantasy* album, in hopes of reviving his career.

Tragedy struck one final time on December 8, 1980. As John and Yoko were returning home after working on tracks from the album, Mark David Chapman shot John Lennon as Yoko stood by his side. Lennon was pronounced dead upon his arrival at the hospital. A life of tragedy and incredible genius had ended.

Sense of Humor

A John's sense of humor tends to be:

- Dark
- Cynical
- Sarcastic
- Biting
- Edgy

Do you have a friend who likes to tell racist jokes on Martin Luther King Day during his speech to the NAACP? Does he tell totally inappropriate tales at just the wrong time (like the one about the hookers at your grandmother's birthday dinner)? Maybe you've been to a party where someone made overly cynical or insensitive jokes. Maybe the humor is insightful and biting, but a tad too angry for polite society. If so, you've probably encountered Johns and their unique sense of humor.

While Johns are known for being more serious people, they also have a great penchant for humor—albeit, dark, cynical, and often mean. Since Johns tend to see the world pessimistically, their humor tends to focus on what they see as a decaying and decadent society, hell-bent on destroying itself. Johns have a tendency to mock culture, especially the more idiotic aspects. So, people who enjoy collecting Beanie Babies or dance the Macarena are often offended by Johns. Most Johns can barely tolerate fools, which tends to lead to jokes and put-downs. For instance, if you find yourself being mocked for wearing your Bluetooth in the grocery store, you probably just encountered a John. Johns also tend to be insecure. Therefore, much of their humor can be seen as a defense mechanism.

At their core, Johns love to make people laugh. This is partly because they prefer to be the center of attention and partly because they want everyone to see how brilliant and witty they are. Being funny is only half as important to a John as being noticed.

While Georges can also be highly cynical humorists, Johns frequently use their humor to challenge people. They aren't afraid to use foul language and stereotypes in order to make a point. To many, just the mention of the N-word makes them uncomfortable, but Johns aren't afraid to use language as part of a larger commentary. To them, the best humor is just a few shades away from an angry rant.

Romance

Romantically, Johns tend to be:

- Compulsive
- Codependent
- Distant (depending on the lover)
- Emotional
- Caring
- Loving

To summarize Johns and their romantic lives, we've got one word: Yoko. Needless to say, Johns are not known for their wise romantic decisions. They are often prone to codependence and picking mates who encourage their worst qualities. However, if Johns make informed decision, they often choose partners who challenge and encourage them. Again, the duality of Johns manifests itself in every aspect of their personality.

When Johns fall in love, they tend to jump off the proverbial cliff with both feet. Have you ever known a buddy to fall madly in love with a girl after the first date? If so, he might be a John. When Johns fall in love, their romance takes center stage, causing them to neglect other aspects of their life. Johns can quickly become codependent with their partners. So, if your girlfriend is constantly calling you on a Friday night while you are out with your buddies, you're probably dating a John.

Johns are also prone to latching on to their partner's terrible qualities and bad habits. Many Johns' drug addiction stems from the fact that their significant other got them hooked. And most Johns weren't really interested in performance art until their girlfriends convinced them to dance naked, covered in peanut butter, in front of a live audience. On the positive side, many wives may never have considered kayaking or mountain biking until they met their John husbands. Johns like to be dominant in the relationships and do *what they want*. It's not that Johns aren't open to new things. They are. It's just that a John's life tends to be more exciting than his or her partners.

While Johns are often attracted to "Yoko" lovers who nurture their worst qualities, this Beatle Sign is also prone to dating and marrying a "Cynthia." Cynthia Powell became John Lennon's first wife after the two discovered she was pregnant. John often felt forced into the marriage and treated Cynthia accordingly, having a number of affairs including one with Yoko Ono. Growing tired of having his infidelity thrown in her face, Cynthia divorced John in 1968. Consequently, Johns have a tendency to find themselves in loveless marriages. Occasionally, through pregnancy or other family expectations, Johns feel a lover might be forced upon them. Unfortunately, when Johns don't care about something, their apathy is often quite obvious. In these cases, this Beatle Sign has been known to trample their partner's feelings and belittle them.

Not all of a John's romantic qualities are negative. When Johns pick correctly, they are often attracted to people who are independent and intelligent. Male Johns are much more likely than other signs to pick female partners who are more of an equal than the stereotypical "little lady." Since Johns tend to fly in the face of convention, they don't like the housewife type or "Girls Gone Wild" bimbo. Female Johns frequently pick men who treat them as equals. They detest the stereotypical subservient role of women in society and seek men who are nontraditional. If Johns can survive their first few marriages, they often make a great third or fourth spouse.

Despite what many assume, Johns are highly affectionate people. They enjoy hugs, hand holding, and snuggling. Johns like to feel close and intimate with people through physical contact.

Family

Johns as family members often are:

- Dedicated
- Unyielding
- Stifling
- Close

For the most part, Johns make loving and dedicated family members. John Lennon was beloved by both his aunt Mimi and his mother. He shared a close relationship with each that went beyond a typical mother/son connection. Many Johns enjoy a close-knit, intimate family. It is their support system, the only aspect of life they feel they can count on. From an early age, John also had a borderline adult relationship with his Aunt Mimi. Since Johns do not usually have a large group of friends they can confide in, they tend to be close to their family members. Johns are most comfortable with their family and trust them with their most intimate thoughts.

Johns also make excellent, dedicated parents. While the real John Lennon was a somewhat absent father in the life of his first son, Julian, which he deeply regretted, John dedicated the last part of his life to raising his second son, Sean. Johns, both male and female, love their children and take the role of raising them quite seriously. They can be creative parents, often designing days filled with fun, athletic, and artistic activities for their children. Johns are more likely to take their child to the zoo or museum than an amusement park. While they are loving, they rarely spoil their children materialistically. As they grow older, Johns also tend to connect with their children as friends and foster relationships that last a lifetime.

Johns put a great deal of trust into their family members. They rely on them to provide stability in their often-chaotic lives. Johns frequently use their home as an oasis away from an exhaustive work environment. To them, family and home are a sanctuary and a place to get away. Johns' spouses need to keep their home a calm environment. If Johns constantly come home to screaming fights and filthy, unwashed kids running around in dirty diapers, they will be tempted to run off with a stripper from Kansas City.

Unfortunately, Johns can be absent from their family if they feel the situation is too stifling. Many Johns ditch their spouses and children to pursue an unfettered life. Johns hate to feel tied down, unless *they* choose it. They are not above simply walking out on their kids and changing names to avoid child support payments. Georges and especially Pauls who are married to Johns need to give their spouses a certain degree of freedom. This may come in the form of them going out to lunch with friends, going camping with a buddy, or some time to play the guitar for a few hours to relieve stress.

Work

Johns in the work setting are often:

- Dependable
- Hard-working
- Inflexible
- Lazy
- Apathetic

In the work setting, Johns can make great bosses, dependable coworkers, and excellent partners. Unfortunately, they can also make slave-driving bosses, pushy coworkers, and know-it-all partners.

Johns tend to have a strong work ethic, making them great employees. They take their work seriously and get it done on time, even if it means stepping on people's toes and staying at work until one in the morning. This is one of the reasons Hollywood and the corporate world are filled with Johns. They want to be the best at what they do.

If you're lazy and don't mind others doing your work for you, Johns make great coworkers. Johns will take over projects to insure success. But in return, they want it done their way. Johns are also notorious for being inflexible. While John Lennon and Paul McCartney created some tremendous music together, their inability to compromise led, ultimately, to their breakup. Johns like to have things their way.

With their biting sarcasm, Johns also bring a huge amount of levity to any stressful or dull work environment. John Lennon had a notoriously dark sense of humor and was known as a prankster in his youth. Johns enjoy a good joke and often exhibit these qualities in the workplace. If left unchecked, Johns can mock and belittle coworkers in a borderline abusive manner. If they keep their humor under control, other employees will appreciate their viewpoint and flippancy.

As bosses, Johns have many positives and negatives. In management positions, Johns are not afraid to get their hands dirty and pitch in. This can make them very popular bosses. They aren't against helping with spreadsheets or staying on hold with India for five hours to solve a computer problem. Again, their need to get the job done correctly can override their desire to be a domineering boss. Since Johns are thoughtful, they often bring new and exciting ideas to the table (like power naps and weekly massages at work).

The negatives depend on your Beatle Sign. Since Johns have such a Puritan work ethic, they can be neurotic, slave-driving bosses who expect you to neglect your family if that's what it takes to land the Peterson account. As bosses, Johns are frequently moody. One day they might praise you for repairing the company server, and the next scream at you for coming in two minutes late from lunch. Employees should learn to spot this moodiness and avoid their John bosses at all costs. As seen before, Johns can be mean SOBs, especially when they are in a position of power. Johns in management can be downright cruel. They will think nothing of belittling a worker who isn't pulling his or her weight.

Ringos should avoid working for Johns if at all possible. Since Ringos have a very different view of work, their skills will not be appreciated. Johns often have a hard time understanding that Ringos don't equate spending the most hours at work with being the most productive.

There is a flip side to Johns at work; call it the "anti-John" John. Remember, Johns can be notoriously cynical. Therefore, if they determine that their work has little value to them personally, they tend not to give a damn. A John's work ethic applies to anything he or she deems important, from the office, to school, to artistic endeavors. So, a John may dedicate himself to his band but completely neglect his job as a barista at Starbucks. Johns like this will do the bare minimum it takes not to get fired. They will often be competent workers, but deep down they don't care whether the place burns to the ground or not. It's important to look for this trait in a prospective employee. If you hire the John, and he doesn't give a crap about the job, be prepared to nail everything down or he's going to rob you blind.

World View

A John's world view tends to be:

- Cynical
- Superior
- Jaded
- Empathetic

Johns are cynical about the world around them. They see hypocrisy everywhere. They often feel as if they are "surrounded by idiots." They also feel the world is in decline (and they're probably right). Johns are pessimistic by nature but nevertheless often try to change their world or community.

Johns have a tendency to have a superiority complex, often feeling they are more intelligent, more worthy, and just plain better than those around them. While this may be accurate, it can often alienate them from their fellow humans. Although Johns feel sympathy toward others and try to right wrongs, they mostly view themselves as separate from the huddled masses.

Beliefs

As with all signs in the Beatle-verse, Johns are highly complex individuals. Not every John will exhibit all of the traits of this sign, but there are several clues that can help you identify yourself or others.

More than any other Beatle Sign, Johns possess a healthy (or unhealthy) dose of cynicism. Johns think the world is falling apart and will disintegrate into a chaotic mess of food riots, epidemic diseases, and unending wars. And that's their optimistic view.

Somewhat related to their general sense of cynicism is their complete and utter rejection of trends and hip culture. Johns *hate* anything trendy. They can't stand trendy music, trendy clothes, trendy food, and trendy gadgets. Johns despise reality TV and remakes of superhero movies. Johns don't camp out in line for two days to see the new *Indiana Jones* movie. Johns don't get tattoos and smoke cigars just to seem cool. And Johns definitely don't rush out to buy an iPhone, quote Snoop Dogg lyrics, buy bug-eye sunglasses, or get custom rims for their Honda. Johns simply detest the hip scene. Unlike Georges, Johns are not silent about their indignation. They will voice their opinions quite emphatically, often alienating their friends or anyone within ear-shot. Johns need to be careful about voicing their disgust for all things trendy as it can get them in trouble at work or with friends. While the occasional barb at Britney Spears is acceptable, a John must realize her criticism can cut too close to home.

Johns and religion are an odd mix, helping to make this the most inconsistent sign in Beatleology. Some Johns despise religion and consider it "opium for the masses." These Johns are openly hostile toward organized religion and its followers. Interestingly, many Johns consider themselves highly religious. They are regular churchgoers and feel

God takes a central role in their lives. How is this dichotomy possible? While a John's attitude toward religion is environmental, the constant is a John's dedication to his or her beliefs. A non-religious John believes it with every ounce of his body. A religious John is just as sure in his beliefs.

Johns and Insanity

Unlike the other signs in Beatleology, Johns have a propensity to go insane. After all, you can't have a "mad genius" without the "mad" bit. And for Johns, this is an unfortunate fact of life, which they must learn to combat. A John's insanity often first manifests itself as various manic and depressive moods. Johns can be incredibly charming one minute and down in the dumps the next. It's not odd to see your John friend be incredibly amiable one minute and pick a fight with your grandmother the next. A John in this stage is often unpredictable. The problem is Johns like it like this. They pride themselves on being unlike other people and not one of the "idiots." To them, being a little abnormal is normal. So, it's hard for Johns to see when they have crossed the line. They need to trust in friends and family members to tell them when they've gone too far over the edge.

Like Lennon, Johns are also prone to substance abuse, which only compounds their mental health issues. It's important for Johns and their significant others to keep an eye on alcohol intake along with anything else they might be ingesting.

47

Johns Throughout History

John Lennon was not the first John on Earth. There were Johns before him and there will be Johns after him. Like the Buddha, archetypal Johns appear every few thousand years as an example to humans. In the future, another John will be born to teach the world the truth of Beatleology. Here are some famous Beatles and how their John sign affected their actions and world history.

Julius Caesar

Caesar was the typical John. He thought he could take over the world (and he did). He thought he was a god and, just like John Lennon, was assassinated. What more do you want?

Van Gogh

Vincent Van Gogh was the mad genius who painted, starved and suffered for his art, and then painted some more. He lived life with the passion and intensity of a John.

Woody Allen

While most might not see Woody as a John, he has a number of John-like qualities. Most obvious, Woody has made some terrible mistakes with women. His relationships are destructive. He's brilliant and definitely has a cynical take on the world. Put it all together and Woody Allen is a John.

Michael Jordan

Jordan is a prime example of a sports John. While he may not be the sharpest knife in the drawer, Jordan has exhibited many John qualities in his professional and private lives. First and foremost, Michael Jordan is incredibly conceited (I guess he hasn't seen himself play baseball). He has stated that he single-handedly won all of those championships and is God's gift to basketball (and endorsements).

FAMOUS JOHNS

Mark David Chapman	Che Guevara
Yoko Ono	Diana Ross
Nelson Mandela	Edgar Allan Poe
Richard Nixon	Ernest Hemingway
Bob Dylan	Joseph McCarthy
Gary Oldman	Oliver Stone
Sean Penn	Denzel Washington
Trent Reznor	Jim Henson
Ted Bundy	Stanley Kubrick
Charlie Chaplin	Al Pacino
Walt Disney	Frank Sinatra
Malcolm X	Eleanor Roosevelt
Queen Elizabeth	Michael Jackson
Judy Garland	Napoleon
Gloria Steinem	

Chapter 4

INNER PAUL: I WANNA HOLD YOUR HAND

Are you an idealist? Is someone you love an idealist? An optimist? A passionate lover? Someone who throws himself into her career, volunteer work, and personal life? Do you think life is wonderful and full of beauty? Maybe you dedicate yourself to your spouse or partner, always wanting to be together. Do you like to express yourself through poetry or sculpting, even if it is a little trite?

Are you sometimes pushy or overbearing? Do you view yourself as attractive and everyone else as an ugly, fat slob? If you answered yes to many of these questions, there is a very strong possibility you are a Paul.

Pauls are often viewed as the second-most dominant sign in Beatleology. If Johns are the dark sign, Pauls should be seen as the light. However, they are not complete opposites. Pauls are often one of the easiest signs in Beatleology to spot. Yet, they are occasionally mistaken for Ringos due to their positive nature.

IDENTIFYING A PAUL: A QUICK CHECK

Are you a Paul? Find out if the following examples describe you or a loved one.

- ☐ You often work overtime and expect others to as well.
- ☐ Expressing yourself is important to you. You have many ways of expressing your thoughts, feelings, and emotions—through writing, music, fine art, or performing arts.
- ☐ You tend to enjoy trendy and fashionable things (like Twitter, SUVs, and Facebook).
- ☐ You are often aggressive and very assertive.
- ☐ You like to stand out and be the center of attention. You are often at ease in large groups or parties.
- ☐ You are very optimistic.
- ☐ You are a dedicated lover or spouse, sometimes too codependent. (You feel distraught when you don't get five text messages from your boyfriend each day.)
- ☐ You are overly critical of others, especially those you see as beneath you.

☐ You want people to have an extremely positive opinion of you.

☐ You take things seriously when others could care less. (Don't they realize the Peterson Account is the most important thing in the world!?)

☐ Your public or professional persona is different from your true self.

☐ You have a romanticized notion of love

What Does It Mean to Be a Paul?

For the most part, Pauls tend to be optimistic, positive people with seemingly boundless energy. They take life very seriously along with their role in it. Pauls tend to be highly successful, thanks to their vigor and competitive nature. However, this desire to succeed can often rub people the wrong way, especially Georges, since Pauls are not afraid to step on other people's toes to achieve their goals. Pauls can also be the loudest complainers in the room since they feel their desires or problems take precedent over others' concerns. For example, if everyone in the office needs a new computer, it's going to be a Paul who complains the most to make sure he or she is first in line for a new laptop. But in some cases, he should be the first one. If anyone is going to get a project in on time and under budget, it will be a Paul. While both Johns and Pauls have strong work ethics, a Paul is more likely to be a successful CEO or manager while a John is more likely to join the Peace Corps.

Pauls' optimism reaches into many aspects of their lives. They see the world through rose-colored glasses. They are romantics. They are confident. They enjoy being the "beautiful people." They tend to embrace hip causes. Pauls will tell you what was on Oprah yesterday or know the lyrics to all of the current Top Forty hits. They've tried all the popular diets and tacked Anne Geddes calendars up in their cubicles. A Paul's optimism should not be confused with that of a Ringo. Ringos tend to have considerably more inner peace and a *c'est la vie* attitude.

Like Paul McCartney, Pauls are usually intelligent. Often their smarts are inherent and intuitive. Pauls can succeed in academia but prefer other paths. Pauls tend to be the artist, not the art history professor. Pauls are not cerebral; instead, they approach life through intuition. They make good corporate executives, not research scientists.

 ## Positive Characteristics

Enthusiastic
Positive
Energetic
Cutesy
Sentimental
Giving
Perfectionist
Contemplative
Optimistic
Popular
Thoughtful

Although not especially deep in philosophical terms, Pauls are highly sentimental. This sentimentality can be seen in both their romantic and artistic endeavors. If you get six dozen roses and an original poem spelled out in tiny shells for Valentine's Day, good chance you're dating a Paul. If you painted a landscape of the New

Jersey skyline because you thought it was so beautiful, you're probably a Paul. Like Johns, Pauls believe everything they do is cute, brilliant, or wonderful. Sometimes they need someone to tell them it's just a damn macramé scarf and not the *Mona Lisa*.

Paul was the cute one. He was universally loved by women all over the world. Fittingly, Pauls all over the world have a strong romantic streak, even to a fault. They make great partners, but can be too caught up in a relationship.

 ## Negative Characteristics

Corny

Overbearing

Narcissistic

Superficial

Power hungry

Overly competitive

Highly critical

Tactless

Demanding

Pretentious

Pushy

Paul McCartney's Life

There are several consistent aspects of Paul McCartney's life. First, he has always been highly driven to succeed and works tirelessly. Since his teenage years, Paul has been churning out music from rock-and-roll to symphonies and toured the world many times over. Second, Paul's life has been filled with strong, supportive women whom he loves dearly but eventually loses. Despite suffering crushing blows with the loss of his mother, Mary, at an early age and later his wife, Linda, Paul maintains an open heart. Paul, like all Pauls in Beatleology, is a multidimensional figure who is often hard to understand.

Like many Pauls, Paul McCartney's strong personality manifested at an early age. Pauls often bond closely with their parents, and they expect other relationships to be as close. Similar to John Lennon, Paul suffered a family tragedy early in his life. But unlike John, the death of his mother left Paul's heart desiring the love he had felt as a boy.

James Paul McCartney was born in Liverpool, England on June 18, 1942. Thanks to his mother's position as nurse and midwife, Paul's birth was handled by a team of maternity nurses who ensured the soon-to-be much-loved boy came out just fine. Mary often worked long, exhausting hours as a nurse, but that didn't prevent young Paul from becoming extremely emotionally attached. A great deal of Paul's work ethic could be attributed to his mother. Paul's father, Jim, was also highly supportive and loving. However, he often had trouble caring for his family in the postwar economy. Luckily, Mary had steady employment as a nurse.

As a child, Paul and his younger brother Mike were often described as a "circus," terrorizing their overworked parents. Like all Pauls, McCartney was full of energy. He often got into trouble but could charm his way out with his adorable face and dreamy eyes.

Early in Paul's life, his family moved to a small but comfortable house in the suburb of Speke. Despite being only a few miles south of Liverpool, to the McCartney clan, it might as well have been a thousand. Notwithstanding their solid blue-collar status, Paul's family strived to be something more. Mary and Jim knew the key to the middle class was through education.

Luckily, Paul was a very bright child and a quick study. At the age of eleven, Paul took the highly selective eleven-plus exam, which determined who would move on to a grammar school (the equivalent of a college-prep high school). Out of the several hundred boys who took the test, Paul was one of four who passed. Paul enrolled in the Liverpool Institute in 1953 at the ripe old age of eleven and had trouble adjusting at first. Despite taking courses in various languages and literature, Paul discovered his love of art, especially drawing.

When Paul was in his early teens, Mary's health began to fail. At first, she chalked it up to indigestion and exhaustion. But as a highly skilled nurse she knew better. Mary was later diagnosed with breast cancer. During her mastectomy, doctors discovered her cancer had spread and the prognosis was grim. Young Paul and Mike saw their mother one more time before she died in the hospital from complications due to the operation. The first love of Paul's life had passed, leaving a giant hole in his heart. For weeks afterward, Paul was like a ghost, completely crushed by the death of his mother.

His one salvation was music. In his younger years, Jim McCartney had been quite the semipro musician. He was self-taught on the piano and had spent much of his twenties playing with big bands or jamming late into the night. At one point, Jim led his own band, the Masked Melody Makers, which later evolved into Jim Mac's Jazz Band. Unfortunately, Jim's music career waned as his professional career took off. But his love of music stayed with him through his years as a father.

Whether it was Jim taking the boys to see a concert or listening to old records, the McCartney household was always filled with music. Eventually Paul was given a trumpet, which he took to enthusiastically, but like most boys in the age of Elvis what he really wanted was a guitar. Paul convinced his father to trade in the trumpet for a cheap guitar made by Zenith. Instantly, Paul found what he wanted to do with his life: rock-and-roll. In typical Paul fashion, he dedicated himself to his instrument.

Unlike most moments in rock mythology, when Paul McCartney met John Lennon, it truly was like a lightning strike. The two teenagers formed a quick bond over their passion for music but also over the loss of their mothers. Interestingly, both Mimi, John's aunt, and Jim, Paul's father, warned their sons about the other boy. To Jim, John Lennon would lead their sweet Paul astray. Aunt Mimi felt Paul's working-class roots were beneath John. To the boys, it didn't matter.

With his superior guitar technique, Paul quickly earned a space in John's band, the Quarrymen. It quickly became John *and* Paul's band, as both made all artistic decisions for the group. Soon Paul brought George Harrison, his friend and guitar virtuoso, into the group. Surprisingly, Paul's relationship with George would later turn south and become the most strained of the group.

The band began gigging around Liverpool in the late 1950s but was considered too rough and amateurish to play the best venues. In 1960 and 1962, the newly renamed Beatles played in small clubs in Hamburg, Germany, where they really started to gain their rock-and-roll chops. After being temporarily deported for "arson," Paul and the band returned to Liverpool where they realized they sounded like every other rock cover band. To set themselves apart, Paul and John began writing original material.

After the death of Stuart Sutcliffe and Ringo Starr's addition to the lineup, the Beatles released their first single, "Love Me Do," in late 1962 with Paul singing the chorus. During the early years of the Beatles, Paul and John cowrote many of their early hits. However, after gaining more confidence, Paul quickly realized he was a talented composer in his own right, often writing hit songs for other performers.

The Beatles' rise to superstardom is one of the greatest rock-and-roll stories—and Paul McCartney takes center stage in that tale. Throughout the 1960s, Paul and the Beatles created some of the most memorable music of the twentieth century. Paul wrote monumental hits such as "Yesterday" and "Hey Jude" and helped create some classic albums like *Sgt. Pepper's Lonely Hearts Club Band* and *Abbey Road.*

Despite Paul's propensity toward love and intense romantic relationships, he was the last Beatle to get married. Although he dated actress Jane Asher throughout the mid-1960s, he eventually married American photographer Linda Eastman. From then on, the two were inseparable. There has been much speculation about their relationship as of late, but one cannot deny they truly loved each other.

The relationships within the group were far from perfect, however. George Harrison temporarily quit the group after growing tired of Paul's dominance and perfectionism. The truth was, despite his puppy dog looks and cute persona, Paul had quite the strong, dominating personality. The success of the Beatles only added to his ego and tendency to control a situation.

On April 10, 1970, Paul announced the Beatles were officially breaking up. One of the greatest eras in rock music had ended, and one of the worst had just begun with the 1970s and McCartney's band Wings. With able help from Linda on the tambourine and triangle, Paul created such hits as "My Love" and "Band on the Run." More important to Paul, he was firmly in charge.

Throughout the 1970s, 1980s, and 1990s, Paul continued his solo career composing everything from rock to symphonic music. Over the course of his career, Paul has sold over 100 million singles and had twenty-nine number-one hits. While John is often seen as the more "artistic" of the two, Paul disagrees with that conclusion. His music, and strong personality, often pushed the boundaries of the Beatles' musical abilities. His influence on popular music is deep and unfathomable. Paul McCartney's music will inspire for generations to come.

Sense of Humor

A Paul's sense of humor is often:

- Mainstream
- Cute
- Cutting
- Lacking
- Trite

Pauls are not known for their senses of humor. In fact, despite their cheery public personas and need to be the center of attention, Pauls don't have a penchant for comedy. Sure, Pauls love to forward funny e-mails or repeat some of Dane Cook's incredibly insightful observations, but deep down, they usually aren't very funny. Part of this stems from the fact that Pauls lack a good sense of the absurd. They take life very seriously and don't see the irony in the way a John might. At its roots, comedy is often criticism. And since Pauls have a strong sentimental streak, they are less likely to be critical of their work, themselves, or life in general. When they do enjoy humor, it is rarely satire. Pauls simply don't see what is so funny.

Pauls will repeat jokes to gain attention, but they are not inherently funny in the same way a John or George might be. They may incessantly repeat lines from the last episode of *Two and a Half Men* or pass "racy" birthday cards around the office. But that is often the full extent of their humor.

When Pauls do use humor, it is often at the expense of others or to pull the focus back to themselves. Pauls hate not being the most important person in the room. To them, a well-placed joke or barb at someone else's expense is all they need to get everyone's attention back where it should be—on them.

Since many Pauls see themselves as cute and adorable, they feel their humor should reflect that. Pauls like to keep it light and rarely risk offending anyone in the group. Pauls want to be fun, not necessarily funny.

Romance

Romantically, Pauls tend to be:

- Sentimental
- Loving
- Compassionate
- Codependent
- Needy
- Romantic

Do you know people who are constantly in love? Skipping from boyfriend to boyfriend, or girlfriend to girlfriend? Were you the girl in high school who was an emotional wreck after your boyfriend of two weeks dumped you for another chick in biology class? Maybe you are the guy who likes to write your girlfriend poetry. Do you have a coworker who swears she just met Mr. Right during her last round of speed dating? Do you know someone who can't be single, even for a month? Chances are most everyone knows a Paul or two.

At their core, Pauls are inherently romantic and loving people. Much of their happiness revolves around their love lives. For a Paul to be content or have a sense of inner peace, they must be either married or in a dedicated partnership. Pauls will often feel incomplete without that partnership. To many non-Pauls, this drive to be in a relationship no matter the cost may seem a bit odd. Simply put, Pauls are lovers. They cannot function without love. Pauls are hopeless romantics—and they are annoyingly codependent girlfriends, boyfriends, and spouses.

Like Johns, when a Paul falls in love, it is often head-over-heels, call-you-every-five-minutes, practice-signing-my-name-with-your-last-name kind of love. The term *love at first sight* was probably written about a Paul. Many Pauls want to believe in true love and being married happily ever after. Sadly, in modern times, "until death do us part" is an unrealistic expectation. Pauls need to feel secure in their love and relationship, often at the expense of their friends and careers.

Unfortunately, Pauls have a nasty tendency of becoming codependent and overbearing in a relationship. They need to not only feel but give love constantly. They need constant reassurance from their partners. Pauls must know what their partner is doing at all times of the day, every day. If a Paul is dating, he may annoy his partner with endless e-mails, text messages, IMs, and voicemails. Pauls want to be in constant contact with their lover. To the non-Paul in the relationship, this habit can be infuriating and possible grounds for divorce. Non-Pauls need to recognize the Paul's need to feel wanted and loved. Inversely, Pauls need to realize that just because they don't get a text message, it doesn't mean their boyfriend has run off with a gymnast.

Interestingly, Pauls are not usually highly sexual people. Sex is more of a means to an end than an end itself. This is especially true for female Pauls. Many female Pauls might be considered sexually aggressive, open, or slutty, but that is often a misconception. In truth, Pauls approach sex as a way of pleasing their partner. For them, sex is a way of getting and keeping a partner. To the untrained eye, they may seem highly sexual, but this Beatle Sign actually uses sex for emotional affirmation rather than pleasure. Male Pauls tend to be subdued in the bedroom. They are often controlling sexually, but they also want their partner to enjoy themselves.

Pauls paired with Pauls in a romantic relationship can work well under the right circumstances. Two Pauls will fulfill each other's need for constant reinforcement and contact. They will enjoy reading each other's bad poetry and looking at their relationship scrapbooks. However, if two Pauls are left unchecked, they can become a toxic mix.

If you've ever seen two awkward adults making out in public like a couple of teenagers, they are probably two Pauls caught up in love. Pauls and Johns can also make for an intense relationship. Both have the tendency to completely throw themselves into a love affair. However, Johns' propensity for over dramatizing can spell doom. Both signs can create an inordinate amount of drama. It's not uncommon for a John-Paul relationship to start as passionate and loving but quickly disintegrate into bickering and verbal abuse. Johns and Pauls can often be heard screaming, "Why won't you let me love you?" at each other.

Pauls should avoid Georges in love. Pauls will resent Georges' inability to commit. They will also resent the ambiguity a George brings to a romantic relationship. A Paul has to know exactly where he or she stands, but Georges don't like to make bold statements of love. On the other side, the George will quickly tire of Paul and find him or her completely annoying. As a general rule, Georges try to avoid overbearing people, especially in their love lives. Georges want partners who are calm and consistent. They can live without the ups and downs.

Paul and Ringo pairings work well in love. Pauls will appreciate the Ringos' ability to go with the flow and let them lead in the relationship. Ringos will appreciate the sex.

Family

Pauls as family members are often:

- Responsible
- Loving
- Idealistic
- Controlling
- Embracing

As with other aspects of their lives, Pauls have a romantic and idealistic view of family life. Whether it is possible or not, Pauls strive to have a traditional, nuclear family. The idea of family brings Pauls comfort and a sense of stability. Pauls want to believe that mom, dad, and kids can be happy. While dating actress Jane Asher, Paul McCartney moved into her family's flat in London. It's hard to imagine most rock stars today living with their girlfriend's parents.

Pauls are attracted to consistency. They like an ordered universe and view family as being at the core of that idea. Family brings comfort to Pauls. They like the concept of their lives being "settled."

In the family setting, Pauls can also be controlling. They tend to set the tone for family events and decide on family activities. Non-Paul spouses need to understand that Pauls need a feeling of control over their lives. It's just their nature to be a little domineering, but they do it with good intentions. In their heart, Pauls want everyone to be happy and in love, but sometimes they can rub people the wrong way in the process. Occasionally, non-Pauls need to step back and allow their Paul spouse to do what he or she needs to do whether it's clean the entire house or watch old family movies. The upside is that he will always remember to pack extra snacks for the kids and plenty of quarters for parking.

Pauls love children and grandchildren. They make loving fathers and mothers. Since Paul McCartney lost his mother at an early age, he understood the effect that could have on a child. Pauls will always be there for their children. They are also strong disciplinarians. Because Pauls have a potent personality and domineering nature, they expect their children to act a certain way. Paul parents set boundaries for their children. They would rather die than allow their children to make a scene in the cereal aisle of the local Wal-Mart. Pauls want their children to be bright, respectful students who will eventually be student body president and valedictorian.

Work

Pauls in the workplace are often:

- Hardworking
- Dedicated
- Intuitive
- Enthusiastic
- Dominating
- Controlling

One thing all Pauls have in common is their strong personality. This fact has positive and negative consequences for both employers and coworkers alike.

First and foremost, Pauls make dedicated, proficient employees. No matter what the job, Pauls are devoted to doing it right. They want to be seen as the best employee or best boss. They are capable and adept at their jobs. To the occasional annoyance of their coworkers, Pauls will arrive at their jobs early and stay late (and let you know it). If you work with a Paul, you need to learn to live with the fact that Pauls also love to complain about how hard they are working, or how hard the Johnson account is compared to your trivial work. A Paul will put in overtime on a project without even being asked. To a Paul, that project *is* their life and they want it done correctly even if it means working fourteen-hour days (interestingly, there are no French Pauls). This is one aspect of Pauls' perfectionism. Since they want everything done right (which, coincidently, is how *they* do it), Pauls can be pushy, rude, and downright mean to those with whom they are working. They are not afraid to insult a coworker or crawl right over their backs to get what they want.

Any work environment needs Pauls. You'll never get anything done with a team of Ringos. Pauls drive the economy. Without them, our economic system would be based around hemp necklaces and esoteric biographies of Bertolt Brecht. We need people who are dedicated to making quality underwear, car brakes, and 747s.

Second, Pauls are generally enthusiastic about their jobs, even if they are working at Hot Dog on a Stick. They truly care about their work. While this trait seems similar to their sense of dedication, it is somewhat different. Johns are also dedicated, hard workers, but deep down, they may not care if their office building gets wiped out in a tsunami. Pauls, on the other hand, *care*. They really want to win DMV Employee of the Month. Success in any form is important to them. A sense of accomplishment is at the core of their identity.

For the other Beatle Signs, there are several annoying aspects of working with Pauls. Pauls have a tendency to be domineering in the workplace. They like things done their way. Their methods are best, which can be especially infuriating for their employees since Pauls can be inflexible. Pauls also have the tendency of dominating meetings, projects, and lunch rooms. They want to be the loudest voice on the conference call. They have opinions about everything and must be on the team-building exercise committee, run the office welcome wagon, and plan the baby showers.

As bosses, Pauls are a mixed bag. On the upside, a Paul won't be your typical lazy-ass boss who takes credit for all of your hard work. A Paul will do his or her own hard work. But Paul bosses can also be highly demanding. They expect the same attitude toward work as they have. Paul bosses can often be heard saying things such as, "You like working here?" or "You like how much you're making, buddy?" (Pauls don't appreciate it if you answer with sarcasm.) They also expect their employees to perform their job the "right way," which just so happens to be their way. Paul bosses like to make executive decisions without input from the team. Georges should avoid working for Pauls as they will resent their pushy and domineering tendencies.

Interestingly, Pauls hate working together and often butt heads. Two Pauls are like two cooks in the kitchen. Each wants to be the best and the center of attention, but that can't happen.

World View

A Paul's world view tends to be:

- Optimistic
- Socially just
- Superior

Despite constant wars, global warming, rising gas prices, and the popularity of *American Idol*, some people seem to keep an optimistic outlook on life. These people are Pauls. Pauls think everything will work out just fine. They may complain, bitch, and moan, but they are very positive people. Pauls believe they can change the world or help push it in the right directions. In politics, Pauls go for the Barack Obamas, Howard Deans, or Ron Pauls, since they believe with all their heart that one person can make a difference. They will devote their lives to saving kids, puppies, or their company.

Pauls have a strong sense of social justice. They believe in right and wrong, and good guys and bad guys. Pauls like to see criminals punished. Pauls also have a sense that right and wrong will work itself out naturally. Cosmically, they feel bad people will eventually get what's coming to them.

Like Johns, Pauls often have a superiority complex. As previously stated, Pauls believe their methods and way of thinking is right and everyone else is wrong (unless, of course, they agree). This sense of superiority can often rub people the wrong way (especially Johns and Georges).

Beliefs

As with most people, Pauls are complicated individuals. A lot goes into being a Paul. While not all Pauls are the same thanks to national, generational, and environmental factors, they all do share many qualities.

Trendy

To put it mildly, Pauls are trendy. They love fashionable clothes, music, movies, and other fads. It makes them feel good to be a part of something, even if it is a fleeting trend. Pauls are often the first person camped out at the local Best Buy to get their hands on a new iPhone or Wii. They know how to do the Macarena. Your Paul friends might have worn WWJD bracelets, which they later traded in for Lance Armstrong bracelets. Many Pauls like sushi and Top Forty music. Female Pauls watch Oprah and read everything on her book club list.

On the upside, Pauls truly enjoy life. They aren't cynical like Johns and Georges and can enjoy things for what they are. Pauls don't need irony to have a good time, they can simply enjoy Disneyland, professional sports, and WWE Wrestling for what it is . . . just a good time.

Religion

While the majority of people claim a belief in God or a higher power, Pauls are the most religious of all Beatle Signs. Since Pauls have a strong belief in good and bad, right and wrong, they tend to trust these ideals were created by a higher power. They like to see the universe as an ordered place, not chaotic and random. Pauls make excellent pastors, monks, rabbis, and reverends as they are often passionate about their beliefs.

While many girls with bug-eye sunglasses at bars will claim to be "spiritual but not religious," this statement is very true for many Pauls. Nonreligious Pauls often claim to be spiritual. This manifests itself in a New Age, Buddhist-lite kind of way. However they act, these Pauls have a hard time believing the universe is just a big accident.

Pauls Throughout History

As with all other Beatle Signs in Beatleology, Paul McCartney was not the first "Paul" on Earth. While he may be the most recent incarnation of the archetypal Paul, others will appear after him to enlighten mankind.

Pauls have had a deep impact on history and world events. Their strong personalities and dedication to their professions have placed them smack-dab in the center of history. This section will explore some famous Pauls and discuss how their Paul Sign affected their actions.

Mark Antony (Marcus Antonius)

Mark Antony helped Caesar conquer Germany and maintain power in Rome. Thinking he could do no wrong, Antony waged a civil war against Octavian Caesar (better known as Augustus) and lost. Despite some personal indiscretions, Mark Antony was a gifted leader and military man. He also had a passionate relationship with Cleopatra of Egypt, which ended in a double suicide (what good relationship doesn't?).

Gary Busey

Gary is an intense and dominating personality. When his acting career began to dry up, Gary turned to fine art where (surprise!) he realized he was a gifted artist.

Bill Clinton

Bill Clinton is a classic Paul. Whenever he enters a room, the focus is immediately on him. People are drawn to his charm and charisma. Clinton has dedicated his life to helping people and he truly believes in his work. And on top of that, he loves strong women (and women, and women, and women).

Jennifer Lopez

Jennifer Lopez is a typical Paul. First, she takes herself much too seriously. (Does the star of *Gigli* really need an entourage of 100 people?) J-Lo thinks her work is very important (apparently, she hasn't seen her own movies or smelled her perfume). Second, deep down, she just wants a story-book romance with Prince Charming.

FAMOUS PAULS

Gerald Ford
Frank Sinatra
Monica Lewinsky
Ronald Reagan
Steve Jobs
Will Smith
Lance Armstrong
Oprah Winfrey
Paula Abdul
Martin Luther King Jr.
Jesus
Martha Stewart

Christopher Columbus
Lyndon Johnson
Magic Johnson
Dog the Bounty Hunter
Elvis Presley
Barack Obama
Robert Kennedy
Nancy Reagan
Rosie O'Donnell
Tiger Woods
Pope John Paul II
Ludwig van Beethoven

Chapter 5

INNER GEORGE: WHILE MY GUITAR GENTLY WEEPS

Are you a calm, contemplative person? Are you shy, yet have an inner strength? Maybe you're well grounded and practical. Do you think you are the only sane person around and everyone else is crazy?

In the office, do you prefer to work independently, not trusting others with your career? Are you passive-aggressive? Do you internalize conflict? Are you a quiet, calculating individual who doesn't act on a whim? Maybe you're an intellectual while despising intellectualism. Could you be an award-winning poet, but you're not willing to take a risk and show your work to anyone? Do people think you're a nice, mild-mannered person, but deep down you're a sexual freak? Is your sense of humor dark and demented, but only a few people know it? If you answer "yes" to many of these questions, there is a good chance you are a George.

Identifying a George: A Quick Check

Are you a George? Find out if the following examples describe you or a loved one.

- [ ] You are often the quiet one at a party. You prefer small groups and more intimate conversation over coffee or drinks.
- [ ] You have different personalities depending on whom you are dealing with.
- [ ] Loud, obnoxious people offend you.
- [ ] You are good at moving in and out of different social circles and groups of friends.
- [ ] You are industrious and hard working to a point.
- [ ] Pretentious, arrogant people drive you crazy.
- [ ] For some reason, you are not good at giving or receiving compliments.
- [ ] You are capable of holding grudges and still get upset about things that happened years ago.

- [ ] Most of the time you are passive, but you can be assertive and aggressive when you need to be.
- [ ] You consider yourself an individual and hate stupid trends. You maintain an anti-style style.
- [ ] You feel you are calm and down to earth while everyone else is insane.
- [ ] You've painted, written books, or composed music for years but have never shown your work to anyone.
- [ ] Usually, you avoid great risk. You prefer a great deal of control over your life.
- [ ] You follow the rules only when they help your cause.
- [ ] You see morality in shades of gray. There are few absolute truths.
- [ ] Your sense of humor is dark and cynical. You often don't share it with people until you get to know them well.
- [ ] You have a small, but intimate group of friends.
- [ ] You consider yourself a strong person and won't allow yourself to be stopped by feelings of depression.
- [ ] You are very astute at observing people.
- [ ] When you are with a lot of people for too long, you often grow tired and need some alone time.
- [ ] You are almost always on time.
- [ ] For the most part, you have confidence in yourself and your abilities, but you prefer to act humbly in public.
- [ ] You work ahead of schedule and always have things completed by their deadline.
- [ ] You are calm, cool, and collected most of the time.
- [ ] Secretly, you feel intellectually superior to most people.
- [ ] You maintain a reputation for intelligence and a calm sanity.
- [ ] You like to make to-do lists to keep yourself on schedule.

What Does It Mean to Be a George?

In a nutshell, Georges are reserved, contemplative, and practical individuals. But they also have a dark side. Despite having a tendency toward being introverted, Georges have a strong independent streak. They won't push too hard, but they prefer to have things done their way. Georges occasionally have social reservations, but in the confines of comfortable settings, they can be quite gregarious and charming. This sign prefers smaller, more comfortable social situations. Part of their social reservation stems from the fact that they are rather guarded about their personalities. Georges often have dark, edgy senses of humor (another similarity with Johns), but they don't immediately share this side of themselves with everyone.

 Positive Characteristics

Creative

Spiritual

Reserved

Quiet

Intelligent

Thoughtful

Insightful

Idealistic

Analytical

Self-disciplined

Reliable

Industrious

Inner George: While My Guitar Gently Weeps

Practical

Introspective

Diplomatic

George Harrison was known as the quiet Beatle. That does not mean he didn't care. In fact, of all the Beatles, he was the most involved with the business side, taking great interest in their finances. Georges tend to be shy, introverted people. They are observers who think before they act or speak (unlike every other idiot who opens his big yap without a thought). Georges are very good at weighing a situation and evaluating people. This is why Georges tend to do well in their careers.

Georges also tend to be intellectual. They frequently spend free time reading, organizing political rallies, wine tasting, or working on artistic endeavors. George Harrison is seen as the most gifted musician of the four. He was truly dedicated to his craft as lead guitarist. Georges like to be good at whatever they do, but in a quiet way. Georges are hard-working employees who rarely make waves. Often very industrious, they can tackle complex tasks and bring projects in on time.

Georges can be very cynical. As a natural observer, Georges tend to see the world as it is: full of idiots and incompetents. However, unlike Johns, they are more at peace with that view and accept life for what it is. They have a dark sense of humor, in contrast to Pauls (another reason they don't get along).

As a group, Georges are more relaxed than other Beatle Signs (aside from Ringos). Georges possess a down-to-earth nature and a sense of realism that Pauls and Johns tend to lack. People who are quick to find easy solutions to problems are often Georges. Georges don't worry; they just roll up their sleeves and get to work. One downside to this inherent trait is that they can often exhibit apathy. To a certain degree, nothing affects a George. They don't get over upset or excited about anything. Occasionally, this lack of emotion rubs other Beatle Signs the wrong way.

Georges are the most introspective sign. Aalways thinking, contemplating, and calculating, they are easily the most philosophical sign. Georges may or may not be religious, but they spend time contemplating existence and trying to find a personal meaning in life. Your college ethics professor was probably a George or at least had a George Minor Sign.

Georges also have a tendency to be followers if they don't assert themselves. If they aren't careful, Georges might find themselves robbing a liquor store if their Paul girlfriend pushes hard enough. Or they might spend their tax refund on margaritas and a flat screen TV if their Ringo husband insists. Georges also need to make sure their voice is heard in their workplace or in their relationships. It's easy for Georges to sit on the sidelines and observe, but they can also miss the boat if they don't speak up.

 ## Negative Characteristics

Shy
Passive-aggressive
Withdrawn
Secretive
Resentful

Jealous
Overly serious
Indirect
Deceptive
Vindictive
Stubborn
Arrogant
Stingy
Cynical
Unassertive
Apathetic

Thanks to their passive nature, Georges get along well with Johns and Ringos. Georges and Johns tend to share a similar sense of humor and cynical outlook. Georges also enjoy Ringos for their carefree attitude and ability to loosen up. Sometimes it takes a Ringo and a Hawaiian shirt to lighten things up and allow a George to loosen his tie.

Georges and Pauls, on the other hand, are a completely different story. In work and romance, Georges can quickly grow tired of a Paul's need to take the lead. Many Georges resent their Paul boyfriends for dictating every date or activity. In this case, the George needs to communicate she doesn't like to go bowling every single Saturday and may enjoy a night at the opera. Obviously, some Georges and Pauls have learned to get along. Under the right circumstances, the two signs can work, but it's important for a George to understand a Paul's need to be in charge. Conversely, a Paul needs to realize a George may have important ideas to contribute.

George Harrison's Life

Upon his untimely death in 2001, George Harrison's family said of him, "He left this world as he lived in it: conscious of God, fearless of death, and at peace, surrounded by family and friends." George Harrison was all those things: a well-liked, philosophical man who had a real sense of inner peace. He was a quiet, yet complex person who had many different aspects of his personality (like all Georges).

George Harrison was born in Liverpool, England, on February 25, 1943, to an Irish family. Unlike John and Paul, George's family lacked any major drama. In fact, they were quite supportive of young George's interest in the guitar and rock music. (Many Georges in Beatleology benefit from calm, supportive parents.)

Initially, George was an intelligent, gifted student in school. He easily passed his eleven-plus exam allowing him entrance to the exclusive Liverpool Institute for Boys (where Paul McCartney was a student). Despite his innate abilities, Harrison quickly grew bored with school. It also didn't help that he discovered rock music and started playing in a band (the 1950s equivalent of texting and YouTube).

Impressed by his playing, Paul McCartney asked George to sit in with the Quarrymen. While John was impressed with his skills, he initially felt George was too young to be in a "serious" rock-and-roll group. Throughout his career as a Beatle, George would struggle to assert himself in the group partly because he was always the "kid." Luckily, his virtuoso abilities on the guitar could not be ignored.

The close relationship between George and Paul grew strained in the Beatles' recording career. While it was Paul that insisted George be allowed to join the band, he was also the most critical and demanding of his friend. Paul was often cruel to George in the studio, demanding that they perform solos and riffs *his way*. Their disagreements and fighting would continue and eventually lead to George temporarily quitting the band (along with several other threats to quit). After the Beatles broke up, George commented that he wouldn't mind working with John and Ringo again but couldn't see playing with Paul.

George was considered the most musically experimental of all the Beatles. He included sitars in several Beatles songs and became an accomplished slide guitar player.

Along with his musical experimentation, Harrison also went through a great deal of soul searching while playing with the Beatles. This is a trait common to all Georges. He was responsible for introducing the band to transcendental meditation. After coming into contact with Ravi Shankar, George became interested in Hinduism. It is often speculated that he was attracted to the emphasis on meditation and mantras, which were often musical in nature. For George, this Eastern philosophy wasn't just a passing fad. He stuck to Hinduism for the rest of his life and was married in a Hindu ceremony.

After the breakup of the Beatles, George had a prodigious musical output through the 1970s. His album *All Things Must Pass* was the first solo album by any member of the Beatles. He wrote several hit songs for Ringo Starr and performed with John Lennon, Eric Clapton, Badfinger, and many others throughout the decades. In 1971, Harrison organized the Concert for Bangladesh at New York's Madison Square Garden to benefit starving refugees.

Throughout the remainder of his life, George Harrison continued to be a productive musician, composer, and philanthropist. In 2001, Harrison discovered that his previously diagnosed cancer had returned and metastasized. George spent his remaining months saying goodbye to friends, recording music with his son, and getting his affairs in order. After his death in November 2001, his last solo album, *Brainwashed*, peaked at number eight on the Billboard charts. He left the world at peace with his life and his music. His loss was felt by millions of fans all over the world.

Sense of Humor

A George's sense of humor is often:

- Dark
- Cynical
- Edgy
- Restrained
- Dry
- Guarded
- Sarcastic

Did you ever realize that the quiet guy in the office has a really dark and demented sense of humor? Maybe you never expected him to write a cynical e-mail mocking your boss or point out the cutting irony in every stupid situation at work. That quiet one with the sense of humor of Lenny Bruce may be a George.

Like Johns, Georges are a dark sign in Beatleology and their sense of humor follows accordingly. Georges enjoy a strong sense of humor and a deep sense of the absurd. They easily spot irony and find it rather amusing. Due partly to their observer nature, this

Beatle Sign has the ability to stand back from a situation and see the absurdity inherent in it. Georges don't take the world too seriously, so they tend to find comedy in the ridiculousness of it all. They enjoy sarcasm and irony on many levels.

Instead of broad comedies, Georges prefer more subtle fare that makes the same keen observations they make every day. Most Georges will find *Hollywood Squares* incredibly annoying but love old DVDs of Richard Pryor. They despise light and mainstream humor. To them, comedy has to have a strong edge of truth to it.

Many Georges have been known to take a gag too far. However, unlike a John, they are less likely to make a racially charged joke at the BET awards. Which is not to say they are not thinking it. Since they often notice the darker side of life, they can be very cynical and biting with their comedy. Georges aren't afraid of their thoughts. They realize that in an abstraction, ideas like Nazis, rape, and religion are not off-limits to humor. It's not that they believe those situations are funny, but they can divorce themselves from the reality of it. To them, life in all of its awful forms is absurd.

As with other aspects of their personality, Georges can be very guarded about their sense of humor. Since Georges prefer to not make waves, they rarely risk offending others with their ironic, deranged wit. Only when they are truly comfortable with someone do they open up and express their true comedic nature.

Georges make excellent comedy writers but terrible comedians. Since they prefer to work behind the scenes perfecting their craft, Georges are more likely to be comedic novelists than the next Jim Carrey. Besides, they hate that sort of humor anyway.

Romance

Romantically, Georges tend to be:

- Caring
- Dependable
- Monogamous
- Stable
- Distant
- Loving
- Sexually adventurous

Does your girlfriend seem more stable and confident in your relationship than her friends who are constantly freaking out? Is your boyfriend a dependable partner and yet a little naughty in the sack? Do you have a loving relationship that might be lacking some of the fireworks you felt with your last psycho girlfriend who tried to burn down your house? If this sounds familiar, you may be dating a George.

In Beatleology, Georges make the most dependable spouses and romantic partners. They are the least likely of all the Beatles Signs to run off to a Caribbean island with a stewardess they met twenty minutes ago. Georges are caring, sensitive, and stable mates. They make the kind of boyfriend your mother will like. And they make easygoing girlfriends who won't call you every hour when you're hanging out with your buddies at the bar. She won't write your names with hearts around them on every piece of paper on her desk. And she probably won't kill your dog and place his head on a pike when you break up with her.

While Georges make dependable lovers, they can also be a little boring. A George boyfriend will only occasionally send you flowers, and he's much less likely to write trite poetry about your love than a Paul or John. They are capable of love, but usually not mad love. Some Georges may take their partner for granted. This sign won't forget your birthday, but don't expect any blue Tiffany's boxes. Pauls and Johns might not have all of their emotional needs met by their George girlfriend. If you need constant reminders of your love in the form of notes, cards, and teddy bears, it's a good idea not to marry a George (pick a John or Paul instead).

Georges tend to be monogamous either in the context of a marriage or dating. Georges don't need to sleep around to prove anything to themselves, as a Ringo or Paul might. Interestingly, part of their monogamous trait stems from lethargy. Georges like to be in stable relationships. For them, it's not worth rocking the boat for a few laughs with a Hooter's waitress. Also, Georges notoriously hate the "game" of dating. They much prefer to have a significant other and not have to worry about online personals, speed dating, or finding guys in the bar scene.

Did your mother ever warn you that "it's the quiet ones you have to be careful of?" This couldn't be truer of Georges when it comes to sex. Just because they can be shy doesn't mean they aren't passionate. And they love to express that passion in bed. Maybe it's their slightly repressed nature. Maybe it's their easy ability to connect one-on-one with others. Whatever the reason, Georges love sex. This doesn't mean that female Georges are sluts or male

Georges Don Juans. Most Georges only have a handful of partners in their life, but they enjoy jumping in the sack whenever they get the chance.

In romance, Georges pair well with Johns and Ringos. When a George dates a John, the two can be a loving, committed couple, especially if the George can minimize the John's more manic qualities. Georges and Ringos can also have great relationships (not to mention great sex). Both will make a down-to-earth couple that can enjoy each other without all the drama.

Family

Georges as family members are often:

- Responsible
- Stable parents
- Loving
- Back-stabbing

Family is important to Georges. Since Georges prefer to have a small group of intimate friends, they often turn to their family to fill this role. They find comfort in their family and appreciate the stability it brings. A George's stability is especially important in a family with children. First, there won't be many screaming fights that involve throwing dishes. They will solve conflicts by talking it out or ignoring it completely. Second, Georges will feel a sense of responsibility and are more likely to pay their child support than a Ringo or John who just fell in love with their physical therapist. Many Georges prefer small families. Even though a George may love her husband and kids, she will still want to get away from them occasionally. Georges treasure their personal time and space which isn't always easy to find in a large family. Spouses must understand this need.

While not the most openly loving Beatle Sign, Georges do care tremendously. A non-George must understand it is sometimes difficult for Georges to express love, gratitude, and other deeply felt emotions. They can at times be sweet, but not in the way a Paul can.

Georges tend to have a loving relationship with their parents even into adulthood. George Harrison's parents were the only ones among the group to support the Beatles early in their career. Many Georges find this to be the case. Much of their grounded personality stems from the self-esteem inherent in those who have loving parents. As adults, Georges are able to transition their relationship with their parents into something approaching a friendship. They are able to leave behind any baggage from adolescence.

Since Georges are able to operate on the sly, under the radar of many other Beatle Signs, they can be traitors to the family. Georges have a tendency to be self-centered, which can cause them to stab their family members in the back. A George has to be aware of his or her tendency to only act in a way that is advantageous to themselves and take into account those they love.

Work

Georges in the work setting are often:

- Skilled
- Diligent
- Punctual
- Underappreciated
- Reliable
- Apathetic

In the workplace, Georges are often valuable employees who accomplish their work without much fanfare. Most office settings have one; that guy who can buckle down and quietly get his work in not only on time, but early. They don't get caught up in the office gossip. They are reliable, dependable, and do a quality job. Georges tend be highly skilled at their craft or work. Just like George Harrison was arguably the most skilled musician in the Beatles, Georges are capable in their professions. While Ringos and Johns are good at faking their abilities in the workplace, Georges truly are talented at what they do. They take pride in being able to accomplish a job correctly.

Georges are also very diligent and punctual employees. They will always be on time to work or meetings, and their projects or tasks will usually be finished before the deadline. Don't be upset if the George in your office gets her files done before you, therefore, making you look like a complete slacker. It's just their nature. Interestingly, much of their diligence and "get 'er done" attitude stems from the fact that

Georges want their work completed so they can relax. Since Georges can be a bit uptight, they feel more at ease knowing their work is finished. Another workplace trait of Georges is their reliability. Any workplace needs several Georges to get all of the work done correctly, whether it's an office or a fishing boat in the Bering Sea.

While Georges enjoy praise like everyone else, they do not seek the spotlight. Consequently, Georges are often undervalued in the workplace. They don't mind others taking credit for their hard work (unlike a Paul who will announce it to everyone). It's important for companies to recognize a George's contribution.

Unfortunately, Georges often have a know-it-all attitude with regard to their professions. Many Georges have a hard time asking for help or advice. They want everyone to perceive that they have everything under control. This trait can get Georges into a lot of trouble at work if they are in over their head. Simply put, Georges don't like to admit they have weaknesses; to them, asking for help is a sign of just that. Georges prefer careers that offer them a great deal of autonomy and independence. Since this Beatle Sign often does their best work when alone, they should keep this trait in mind when picking a career. Georges do well as college professors, engineers, mechanics, writers, truck drivers, doctors, and computer programmers. Georges prefer to be given a task and then allowed the freedom to complete the project as they see fit. Non-George bosses should be aware of this characteristic and allow their George employee a great deal of leeway. In the end, they will receive a better product than if the boss dictates every aspect of a project. When Georges are micromanaged, they tend to shut down.

Inversely, Georges should avoid a number of careers to which they are ill suited. For example, Georges make terrible salespeople.

They would rather endure a Brazilian wax than have to "sell" something. It's just not in their nature. Georges should also avoid careers such as coaching, human resources, travel agent, stockbroker, and politician.

In the workplace, Georges pair best with other Georges, Johns, and Ringos. Georges paired together accomplish a great deal without annoying each other. Georges and Johns can also work well together since they have a similar sense of humor and world view. A George will need to be aware that the John will prefer to control the situation. Georges and Ringos can also be a productive mix. While a George may complete most of the work, he will enjoy the Ringo's easygoing attitude and the levity she brings to every situation. Georges can work well with Pauls, as long as their relationship has certain boundaries. If their work is not intimately connected, Georges and Pauls can work together, but don't ask them to share an office or work together for days and weeks on end.

World View

A George's world view tends to be:

* Pessimistic
* Peaceful
* Resigned
* Philosophical

Due to their introspective and contemplative nature, Georges have a complex world view. To them, morality is not absolute. They tend to view the world in shades of gray and reject the notion of good guys versus bad guys. For this reason, many Georges are anti-war and anti–death penalty. Georges think that most situations (like war) are complex and require a great level of thinking and evaluating.

Georges can often have a pessimistic nature. Since Georges aren't romantic, they tend to see the negative side of the world. They are often very aware of current events and politics, which fuels their pessimistic fire. Also, by their nature, Georges don't want to get overly excited about anything. They approach life cautiously. Simply put, they don't want to get their hopes up. George Harrison was very optimistic and organized many benefit concerts, but most Georges aren't jump-up-and-down excited about anything.

In all of Beatleology, Georges are by far the most philosophical sign (their attitude toward religion will be discussed in the next section). As previously stated, Georges are contemplative individuals. They are questioners. This often leads them to discussions about meaning and purpose (which can really bore a Ringo at a party). Georges have the tendency to step back and think about their lives or the passing of time. Pauls and Ringos have to realize this isn't meant as a buzz kill, it is just part of their nature.

Georges Throughout History

Georges have made a number of important contributions to world history, politics, and culture. Unfortunately, Georges are often overshadowed by the aggressive nature of the other Beatle Signs. But Georges have been some of our most influential thinkers and thoughtful artists.

John Adams

While more outspoken than most Georges, John Adams exhibited many George-like traits. He was famously pragmatic and yet had high morals and ideals. On more than one occasion, he bumped heads with Benjamin Franklin (a Paul). He was also notoriously cheap. Adams disliked living in the White House because he had to shoulder the expense of the domestic staff and its upkeep (Georges hate to spend money frivolously).

Charles Schulz

The late Charles Schulz's shyness, deep Lutheran faith, and introspective nature made this cartoonist a George. Like many Georges, he was extremely introverted and guarded. He hated being psychoanalyzed through his *Peanuts* cartoons and often kept to himself.

Steve Martin

While many people wouldn't think of this "wild and crazy guy" as a George, Steve Martin exhibits many of this Beatle Sign's traits. First, despite his occupation, Steve Martin can be reserved and thoughtful. He has a cynical and edgy sense of humor. More recently, he's turned to novel and playwriting along with a heavy dose of philanthropy.

Al Gore

Al Gore is a classic George; he's intelligent, analytical, thoughtful, introspective, and philosophical . . . exactly the kind of person we definitely would not want as president of the free world.

FAMOUS GEORGES

Jimmy Carter
Abraham Lincoln
Gandhi
Noam Chomsky
The Buddha (Siddhartha
   Gautama)
Barry Bonds
George Washington
Friedrich Nietzsche
Bill Cosby
Harrison Ford
George Clooney

George Orwell
Edward Norton
Kurt Vonnegut
Chris Rock
Alfred Hitchcock
Thomas Edison
Laura Bush
Bill Gates
Isaac Newton
Jane Goodall
Andy Kaufman

Chapter 6

INNER RINGO: WITH A LITTLE HELP FROM MY FRIENDS

Do you make friends easily and benefit from those relationships? Do people think you are charming and funny in an unpretentious way? Do you put people at ease and allow them to let their guard down? Are your accomplishments and talents sometimes overshadowed by those of your coworkers?

Do you enjoy the finer things in life like food, sex, vacations, and fine wine? Generally, are you at peace with the world? Are you okay with letting others worry about everything? If so, you may be a Ringo.

IDENTIFYING A RINGO: A QUICK CHECK

Are you a Ringo? Find out if the following examples describe you or a loved one.

- [ ] You make friends easily and keep up with friendships.
- [ ] You have a lot of diverse interests, hobbies, and careers.
- [ ] To you, life is what you make of it. Life is like a journey; there are good parts and speed bumps.
- [ ] You are sometimes overlooked for accolades.
- [ ] You're seen as cute but not the most beautiful person in the room.
- [ ] You would rather get along than cause an argument.
- [ ] You are okay being a regular person and don't need to be rich and famous. We can't all be Brad Pitt.
- [ ] You love to party and hang out with popular people.
- [ ] You tend to be a generalist. You're sort of good at a lot of things, but not truly amazing at anything. For example, you are a capable athlete in many sports, but aren't particularly gifted at any one game.
- [ ] You find yourself leering at attractive women even when out with your wife.
- [ ] You measure your words and actions carefully to benefit you the most.
- [ ] You are practical in romance and don't fall head over heels.
- [ ] You are above gossip. Most everyone likes you or can't find a reason not to.
- [ ] You are pragmatic, knowing nothing is all good or all bad.

What Does It Mean to Be a Ringo?

Of all the Beatle Signs, Ringos are the most down-to-earth and often the happiest. They are able to enjoy the simple things in life like home and family. Ringos have a natural sense of humor and charisma that put people at ease. Ringos may not be the center of attention, but their approachability and humility may well make them more popular than those with more dominant Beatle Signs.

 Positive Characteristics

Loyal

Exuberant

Funny

Charming

Appreciative

Popular

Friendly

Humble

Persevering

Forgiving

Fun loving

Ringos tend to be loyal friends and lovers; they are able to form lasting relationships. They are able to accept the good as well as the bad in people. Ringos will avoid confrontations of stubborn egos that can lead to the ruin of a relationship. Familial bonds are important to Ringos and bring them great joy. Unfortunately, so does hedonism. A Ringo may see no incongruity in attending his daughter's church youth choir concert in the afternoon, going to a Rotary Club banquet in the evening, and topping the day off with a booze-fueled swingers party all night.

 ## Negative Characteristics

Underappreciated

Meek

Flippant

Fickle

Shallow

Impatient

Lusty

Hedonistic

Manipulative

Uncommunicative

Really fun loving

Most Ringos are appreciated in the workplace as both coworkers and bosses. Ringos tend to have a positive attitude toward work and their careers, yet they don't get stressed. They get along well with everyone since they are unpretentious and don't step on others' toes. If left unchecked, Ringos have the tendency to become a little lazy. Many need the occasional kick in the pants to stay productive. As bosses, Ringos have their positives and negatives. They make excellent diplomats and are able to defuse tensions between employees. However, they can also be *too* uncritical and not push their employees enough.

Philosophically, Ringos are not the deepest, most thoughtful, or most religious sign in Beatleology. They tend to take life for what it is. A Ringo is not likely to write a treatise on existentialism, but many create a personal philosophy by which they live. Many Ringos are also casually religious. They may believe in God or a higher power but might pick and choose the aspects of their religion that they like or fits their lifestyle. Ringos are rarely fundamentalists or religious extremists.

Ringo Starr's Life

Ringo Starr was born Richard Starkey, named after his father, in Liverpool on July 7, 1940 (the oldest of all the Beatles). As young Richie's mother, Elsie, was lying in bed recovering from the birth, the first air raid sirens of World War II sounded.

When Ringo was three, his parents separated, and Ringo rarely saw his father throughout the rest of his childhood. Ringo grew up in the Dingle section of Liverpool. Despite its funny English name, the Dingle was one of the toughest and most poverty-stricken areas of Liverpool. Like John and Paul, who had lost parents to death, Ringo grew up without a traditional family life. During his youth, Ringo's mother worked as a barmaid and showed the very Ringo-like qualities of enjoying the company of others and benefiting from a funny, charismatic personality.

When Ringo was six, he almost died from a burst appendix. Following two surgeries, he slipped into a coma for ten weeks and was in the hospital for a full year fighting to recover. In those days, parents were not allowed to visit their children in the hospital for fear they would disturb their recovery. This separation at an early age helped form Ringo's appreciation for family as well as his independent nature. Young Ringo found himself far behind his classmates in his studies. Disliking school, Ringo began to cut class, get in fights, and commit petty thievery. Around this time, Elsie started dating and later married Harry Graves, originally from London. Harry's relationship with Ringo was more that of a favorite uncle than a father, Ringo often taking Harry's side when he and Elsie would have the occasional row.

At thirteen, Ringo suffered his second major illness, effusion of the lung, and returned to the hospital for almost two years. During his long convalescence, he was given art supplies and encouraged to creatively occupy his time. The hospital also had a few instruments, including a drum kit. This marked Ringo's first interest in music.

When Ringo left the hospital at age fifteen, his mandatory school days were behind him and he did not have the marks to continue. Elsie worried that young Ringo would have a hard time in the working world. He was too weak and sickly for manual labor and had barely a junior high school education (equivalent to a BA now). After quitting a job as a messenger boy for British Railways, he got a job on a short-run ocean liner as a barman. After six weeks he was fired for showing up drunk to work after an all-night party. At age seventeen, he was able to land an apprenticeship to become a fitter that could have led to a stable blue-collar career.

Then, along with many teenage boys of the era, he was overtaken by the skiffle music craze that hit Liverpool. Suddenly lads with only the most rudimentary musical ability were forming bands and playing local gigs. Ringo helped found a group called Eddie Clayton Skiffle and bought his first drum set for £10.

Eddie Clayton Skiffle played the same small-time club circuit as John, Paul, and George in the Quarrymen. As skiffle gave way to straight rock-and-roll, Ringo joined Rory Storm and the Hurricanes, the area's most successful pop group. Ringo chose to quit his day job and devote himself full-time to being a musician. Eventually Rory's group accepted an extended engagement at Hamburg's Kaiserkeller, where they joined the Beatles playing nightly sets. Ringo made friends with the Beatles, eating and drinking with them between sets and even sitting in with them on the drums once in a while.

Ringo's addition to the Beatles came just before their big break. To many, this fueled the idea that he was one of the luckiest individuals on earth. After Brian Epstein agreed to manage the Beatles and they were set to record their first single, the boys decided to replace Pete Best as the group's drummer. There is much speculation in Beatles lore regarding the reason for this last-minute change, but many say the other members of the band were jealous of Pete's good looks and popularity. If this is the case, then their decision to replace Pete with the talented and affable, but very average looking, Ringo Starr makes a lot of sense. Ringo's easygoing, nonthreatening charisma and ability to make friends catapulted him into a position as one of the all-time top icons of music.

Over the next few years of relentless touring, Ringo went from a good drummer and an add-on to an extraordinary drummer and integral band member. Though he frequently does not receive proper credit, Ringo pioneered a style of drumming for popular music that persists today. Known for his fills and rock-solid beat, he is said to have advanced modern drum technique by leaps and bounds. In later years, many celebrated drummers credited Ringo as their biggest influence. Ringo contributed a fun, baritone, novelty voice to the band, averaging one song on each album. He is also said to be the best actor of the group, taking prominent roles in their movies.

After the Beatles breakup in April 1970, Ringo stayed friends with all three of his former band mates as the others went through a period of anger and squabbling, trading insulting song lyrics in their various solo albums. Ringo frequently worked with John, Paul, and George on various projects, musical and otherwise. Ringo also remained friendly with his former band mate's wives and ex-wives (but not in a bad way), being the only Beatle to fly to New York City to comfort Yoko Ono after John's murder.

In 1975, Ringo divorced his first wife and mother of his three children, Maureen Cox. Starr later "starred" in the 1980 film *Caveman*, which won the Oscar that year for Best Picture to Watch While High. On the set he met his future wife, Barbara Bach, who is best known for the female lead, Agent Triple X, in the James Bond film *The Spy Who Loved Me*. Ringo's son Zak Starkey is also a talented drummer, playing with Oasis and the Who.

Throughout the 1980s, Ringo and Barbara enjoyed a jet-set lifestyle, which involved many celebrity parties and a lot of drinking. Ringo did a brief stint in rehab for alcoholism in 1989 and has since sworn off mind-altering substances.

In the years since the Beatles, Ringo has been engaged in an amazing variety of creative projects including solo albums, acting, producing, live performing, and guest appearances on albums with other musicians.

Sense of Humor

A Ringo's sense of humor is often:

- Lighthearted
- Not at the expense of others
- A tension defuser
- Flippant
- Calculated

When the mood is tense, do you sometimes make a funny quip to lighten things up? Are you cute and cheeky? Are you funny, but not hilarious? Ringo was known as "the funny one," and used his affable sense of humor and likeability to his advantage. People whose Beatle Sign is a Ringo share this trait. When sitting down for a marine corps boot-camp haircut, a Ringo might very well request "just a little off the sides." Before his execution, a Ringo might ask for a doggie bag for his last meal so he can "finish it tomorrow." Ringos are flippant. Ringos are sassy. They are the least serious of all Beatle Signs and have the lightest sense of humor. If Johns and Georges are like George Carlin, Ringos are more like Jeff Foxworthy.

While humorous and entertaining, Ringos aren't necessarily the funniest comedian in your office. Ringos tend to lack the edge that marks the humor or Johns and Georges. Consequently, a Ringo's sense of humor is generally less racist, sexist, and foul than the other signs. This is why your Ringo friend is a good choice to make the toast at your wedding.

In the later years of the band, when personal and creative tensions between John, Paul, and George threatened the well-being of the group, Ringo's lighthearted, optimistic humor helped smooth things out. An individual who is an Inner Ringo can be an excellent addition to any group dynamic suffering from "too many chiefs and not enough Native Americans." Benefiting from this trait is no accident. A Ringo knows that it is in his or her best interest to play the role of the "funny one" who is everybody's favorite.

Romance

Romantically, Ringos tend to be:

- Lighthearted
- Practical
- Flirtatious
- Not smothering

Ringo Starr (or Alpha Ringo) was considered the least attractive member of the Beatles, but he was also the biggest ladies' man. Ringo played in several popular bands before joining the Beatles. As a result, he enjoyed the attention of the ladies who came with it. John, Paul, and George were always obsessed with the idea that their wives and girlfriends loved them for who they really were apart from their fame. Ringo willingly accepted that as a celebrity he could score with girls who would never have given him the time of day when he was a messenger boy earning 50 bob a week. Ringo's first wife, Maureen Cox, was a beautiful young fan caught up in the hysteria of early Liverpool Beatlemania. She fell in love with Ringo before the two had ever met. Ringo's second wife, Barbara Bach, was a hot young B-movie star in a fur bikini on the set of *Caveman* infatuated with the older rock star. Ringo, ever the pragmatist, was willing to take love where he could get it, unconcerned that his fame was part of the equation.

Ringos enjoy a piece of "arm candy," and successful Ringos frequently choose trophy wives as a trapping of their station. Female Ringos also have the tendency to go for the "cutie" over the guy with any substance or the ability to speak in complete sentences. If Ringos are just dating, there is no harm in this preference. But when they look to settle down, Ringos need to consider their choices carefully.

Ringos are very romantic in a fun and flirtatious way, enjoying dating and sexuality. A Ringo's independent nature tends to keep them more realistic in their expectations of a lover. It also helps to steer the relationship away from codependency or obsession. This is in stark contrast to the romantic tendencies of some of the other Beatle Signs. Johns tend to fall "head over heels" in love, sometimes to their detriment. Pauls constantly seek approval and praise from their mates and can feel neglected without constant attention. Ringos are much more secure in their relationships. If a Ringo doesn't receive a nightly call from her boyfriend, she doesn't immediately panic and think the relationship is over. However, Ringos can become too relaxed in their relationship and not put forth the effort to make it work.

Ringos have a strong domestic side and appreciate the stability children and spouses bring. Ringos in committed relationships need to beware of their wandering eye and affinity for short-term passion at the expense of long-term love. Ringos also need to beware of attracting gold diggers or dating hot, psychotic men or women. Many restraining orders are taken out by Ringos, but very few are issued against them.

Family

When it comes to family, Ringos tend to be:

- Permissive
- Warm
- Affectionate
- Easygoing

Ringos tend to take great joy in parenthood. Ringo was an only child and grew up without his father. When the Beatles quit touring, Ringo was able to spend a great deal of time with his three children as they grew up. Now adults, Ringo's kids still enjoy a very close relationship with their father. Zak Starkey frequently plays drums on his father's recordings and live performances.

Ringos tend to see their children more as peers than dependents, which leads to a very friendly, easygoing relationship but can cause problems with lack of discipline. Alpha Ringo had this sort of relationship with his stepfather Harry (also a Ringo), who flatly refused to partake in discipline. Both Ringo mothers and fathers need to learn to set boundaries for their children. The next time you see a child riding his bike in traffic, staring directly into the sun, or running with a fork in his mouth, you're probably seeing the offspring of a Ringo. Ringos should raise children with Pauls or Georges to have the best chance of offsetting these overly lenient tendencies. The Ringo parent will always be the pushover, easily giving permission and forgiving. Their children will quickly learn to go ask Dad if they can meet that "man they just met on the Internet." Ringo parents need to learn to say no.

As spouses, Ringos take a lot of pride in providing a good home and happy existence for their families, often striving to give them what the Ringo lacked in his or her childhood. On the negative side, Ringos have a wandering eye and a fondness for attractive members of the opposite sex (or same sex for gay Ringos, also known as Epsteins). Ringos are the most likely Beatle Sign to cheat on their marriage and the most able to keep it a secret. To a Ringo's mind, there is nothing that says you can't love your wife and family with all your heart and still enjoy the occasional hot Brazilian escort. Ringos also have a tendency to "keep up appearances" when it comes to family life. The guy at the country club with the seemingly perfect wife and children whose family life is secretly like something out of a Tennessee Williams play is probably a Ringo.

Work

Ringos in the workplace tend to be:

- Team players
- Unmotivated
- Peacemakers
- Composed
- Popular

Ringo Starr was known for his rock-solid drumming and playing his instrument the most consistently during Beatles recording sessions. Workplace Ringos are equally consistent in both their positive and negative attributes. Offices and other work environments need Ringos, but there are certain caveats.

In corporate settings, Ringos tend to do their prescribed job well, but sometimes fail to take initiative or go the extra mile. Often this is because they do not get proper credit for their contribution, being overlooked in favor of high-profile Johns or Pauls. Ringos are generally well liked at the office and easily make friends with coworkers and superiors. Office Ringos are frequently invited to golf weekends and expensive corporate dinners well above their pay grade. Frequently, Ringos are seen as all charisma and networking with little actual talent, but this reputation is usually undeserved. This is why Ringos make excellent salespeople, real estate agents, and CEOs. Above all, Ringos are consistent and do not suffer from the highs and lows of a John or, to a lesser extent, a Paul. However, some Ringos are seat warmers and get by on sheer charm and connections.

Ringo bosses are usually good to work for; they will not micromanage or smother the creativity of their employees. Luckily for employees, they aren't slave drivers and won't expect you to miss your son's bar mitzvah to finish a project. Ringo bosses understand the importance of time away from work and the need to have a life outside the office. However, they do sometimes fail to give enough direction or constructive criticism. Of all the Beatle Signs, Ringo bosses are the most likely to give credit to their subordinates for a job well done.

Ringos have a taste for the good life and a tendency to take full advantage of expense accounts, country club privileges, and "business" meetings in the Bahamas. Ultimately, the company benefits from connections and deals made by these perks. This sign should be aware they can be fired if they get too greedy.

Ringos thrive in a work environment based on immediacy, but do not do as well in situations requiring extended periods of tedious concentrated effort for a long-term goal. Ringos aren't suited for computer programming or working in a factory. To be successful, they require a workplace that involves communication and camaraderie. Ringos make good trial attorneys, military personnel, and actors and generally poor researchers, novelists, or academics.

World View

A Ringo's world view tends to be:

- Laissez-faire
- Localized
- Questioning
- Secular

Ringos are generally the most "comfortable in their own skin" of all the Beatle Signs.

They are less driven to change the world and are more concerned with personal ethics. This sign is content living life on his or her own terms. They agree with the old adage that the best people to be in positions of power are too smart to seek it. Our modern heads of state, religious fanatics, and law-enforcement officials, to a Ringo's mind, prove this adage. For this reason, there are few Ringos in politics or powerful religious offices. Jim Jones, of Jonestown, poisoned Kool-Aid fame is a John, willing to kill and die to change the world around him to suit his beliefs. A Ringo would be having too much fun in 1970s San Francisco, smoking weed, discoing, and enjoying casual sex to move to the sweltering jungle of Guiana to brainwash his followers. Ringos care about the world, but they are more likely to lead through quiet example than dramatic action.

While a Ringo is less likely to move to the Sudan to help stop hunger and genocide than a John, this sign is very giving to local causes. Ringos recycle, walk 5Ks for leukemia, and lead the PTA. Many Ringos can be seen beautifying their neighborhoods. Since Ringos like to see the results of their actions, they get more satisfaction out of volunteering locally than writing checks to some charity half a planet away.

Many Ringos are also at peace with the current order of the world. It's not that they enjoy a world filled with people in sad circumstances such as child labor and prostitution, but they seem to believe that "that's the way the world works." This Beatle Sign believes not everyone wants to be saved. It's not that they enjoy being the ugly American either, but a Ringo vacationing in Burma believes she can't single-handedly save everyone from poverty.

Those individuals with an Inner Ringo tend to have a very accepting and inclusive view toward other cultures, religions, and nationalities. A Christian Ringo is likely to see the merits of Judaism, Islam, and Buddhism, whereas a Christian Paul is more likely to damn them all to hell if they don't convert (see Jerry Falwell). Ringos are highly tolerant of others and are content to allow people to live their lives as they choose.

In terms of their religious views, Ringos are often secularists. Many Ringos do not ascribe to any one specific religion. For instance, a Ringo may claim to be a Christian but hesitate to align himself with a particular faith such as Roman Catholic, Baptist, or Methodist. Many hold a notion of a higher being, but also find God in places like nature, their cat, and the world as a whole (like the Force, but only without Jedis). Ringos have a variety of different religious beliefs, but few are religious zealots.

Beliefs

Of all the Beatle Signs, Ringos are the most content. They are able to appreciate what they have and what they have accomplished. Paul McCartney will work his butt off even after he is worth £1.5 billion. Ringo Starr is happy to tour Indian casinos with his friends and host children's shows. Everyday Ringos are also content with their general lot in life. They aren't greedy and willing to step on others' toes to achieve financial success. This isn't to say they don't appreciate the finer things, but Ringos can be happy driving a Toyota Corolla and living in an apartment as long as their life is filled with friends, family, and fun.

Ringos benefit from the fact that, unlike other Beatle Signs, they can really enjoy life. While Georges and Johns will spend all of their free time trying to fulfill some inner need, Ringos will be down at the pub having a pint. Ringos can relax. They can enjoy bad movies and fatty foods. Ringos enjoy going to the dog park or playing Yahtzee. For them, every weekend does not have to be an adventure and every book they read doesn't need to be a Pulitzer Prize winner. When Ringos go on vacation, they truly enjoy it; they don't worry about work or whether they left the iron on. Non-Ringos should follow this sign's example and try to lighten up.

As we've seen, Ringos enjoy fine foods, alcohol, drugs, and meaningless sex. Like Pauls, Ringos can occasionally be trendy individuals. Your Ringo friend probably took to drinking mojitos like a fish takes to water. Many Ringos love good wines and the latest restaurants. Conversely, many Ringos (especially those without the economic means) are able to completely reject trends. Ringos transcend being trendy and hip. Many just don't care. A Ringo of this nature won't care that she is wearing unfashionable clothes. In fact, she might make a joke about it and be proud. These Ringos would rather spend money on several rounds of drinks than a pair of slacks from Nordstrom. If you know an "old hippie" who wears sandals and old, grubby T-shirts, he is probably a Ringo.

Ringos are an essential part of the cosmic order. They provide a reasonable, practical counterbalance to the passionate, sometimes manic, Johns and Pauls and quiet Georges. Individuals who are Ringos should be proud.

Ringos Throughout History

Like Ringo Starr of the Beatles, Ringos have had a profound effect on world history. Although many famous Ringos have not played key roles in world events, they are nonetheless critical to the harmony of the world.

Marie Antoinette

Some Ringos don't have much between their ears and are helplessly caught up in the world of the more powerful people around them. Living a frivolous lifestyle at their expense did not endear her to the angry mobs of pitchfork-wielding French peasants.

Ed McMahon

If ever someone benefited from their ability to make friends and not rock the boat, it was Ed McMahon. The quintessential Ringo, McMahon enjoyed almost half a century of being one of America's most beloved supporting players. He truly was "just happy to be here."

Ronald Reagan

The Great Communicator. Even as he destroyed unions, ran up the national deficit, and helped mega corporations move manufacturing jobs overseas, he was one of the most beloved presidents in history. Reagan's Ringo nature of down-to-earth likeability radically changed the direction of U.S. society and politics.

Ozzy Osbourne

In the 1980s, Ozzy became a scapegoat of the religious right, blamed for everything from promoting devil worship and suicide, to animal cruelty and pissing on the Alamo. Now, through his Ringo-esque qualities of unpretentious likeability, he is seen as the lovable, bumbling (and overly medicated) father figure.

FAMOUS RINGOS

Conan O'Brien

George W. Bush

Tony Blair

Britney Spears

Billy Ray Cyrus

Ted Danson

Paris Hilton

Liberace

Colin Powell

David Arquette

Tommy Lee

Marilyn Monroe

Nicole Richie

Larry Bird

O.J. Simpson

Why Everyone Loves a Ringo

Despite being the least handsome and considered the least musically gifted Beatle, why is Ringo everyone's favorite? Simple. Most of us identify with being average looking and not particularly gifted. Let's face it; we all can't be beautiful and talented. Ringo is the ultimate underdog who made it big. And we love him for it. He is also the most grateful for his career and accomplishments. John, Paul, and George prefer to look down from their pedestals; whereas, Ringo is the most accessible and down-to-earth.

People who are of the Beatle Sign Ringo are frequently also the favorites. They make people feel good about themselves and are supportive friends, coworkers, and loved ones. Ringos enjoy a good time and put others at ease. A Ringo's friendship and love is genuine and easily recognized by others. Ringos are quick to compliment, but think twice about criticism.

Chapter 7

MINOR SIGNS: GET BACK

By now you might be wondering, how can all of the Pauls, Georges, Johns, and Ringos I know be so different from each other? Obviously, all people are complex individuals with a wide array of personalities. So, what accounts for these differences among people of the same Beatle Sign? Simply put, many of us have a Minor Beatle Sign.

Each individual has a major (most prevalent) and a minor Beatle Sign. The minor sign is a small undercurrent of an individual's essence and explains why an individual's behavior might deviate from the characteristics of his Inner Beatle. In short, minors are the exception that proves the rule. Someone might have the major Beatle Sign of a Paul, exhibiting a positive, high-energy perfectionism in public life, and a minor sign of a John that causes quiet reflection at home.

Minor signs are important to us for several reasons. First, they help us understand why our personalities (and those of our friends and family) deviate from our major Beatle Sign. For example, knowing your Ringo boss has a John minor sign will help explain why they have a tendency to be cruel. Or if you're aware that your wife is a Paul with a George rising, you will understand why this usually gregarious woman needs to be alone occasionally.

Most individuals have a minor sign. However, occasionally people are a "pure" sign and only exhibit those traits. It's critical to discover the truth about yourself and your loved ones.

How to Determine Your Minor Beatle Sign

Do you have a minor Beatle Sign? Use this quick checklist to see if you are not a "pure" Beatle.

- ☐ Do you exhibit traits of multiple Beatles?
- ☐ Do you see yourself as one Beatle at work and another in your personal life?

- [ ] Do you have impulses that go against your basic nature? (Maybe you tend to be very health conscious, but occasionally down a pint of Chunky Monkey ice cream.)
- [ ] Do different people in your life see you in vastly different ways? (Your mom thinks you're a Paul, and your boyfriend is convinced you're a Ringo.)
- [ ] Has your personality changed over the years?
- [ ] Do you have a hidden side?
- [ ] Have your interests or careers radically shifted since you were young?
- [ ] Are there many sides to your personality?
- [ ] Do you often have conflicting instincts?

For many, the minor, or "rising" sign, is quite obvious. If you're generally an introverted, thoughtful person, but you like to occasionally cut loose and forget your troubles, you're probably a George with a Ringo rising. But for others, the minor sign is not always so clear.

Like brain surgery, quantum physics, and astronomy, the theory of minor signs is not an exact science. To accurately determine your minor sign, return to your quiz results in Chapter 2. The Beatle Sign that scored the second-most answers is your minor sign. If your results show no clear second-place sign (i.e., the three remaining signs are all within a few points of each other), you do not have a minor and are considered a "pure" sign. It is also important to read the descriptions of each Beatle Sign. Even if you are clearly not a Paul, you still may see some Paul characteristics (and therefore your minor sign).

Incorporating Your Minor Sign into Your Beatleology Lifestyle

Once you have discovered your minor Beatle Sign (assuming you do indeed have one), it's important to learn how the characteristics of that new sign will impact your life. Remember, your major sign is dominant, but your minor sign will also dictate aspects of your behavior and relationships.

John Minors

Individuals with John as their minor will occasionally exhibit both the positive and negative traits of the sign. First, those with John risings often have a hidden, creative side to their personality. For the middle-aged Texas homemaker, that might mean amazing Christmas decorations or scrapbooks. For a Ringo, it might mean a journal of surprisingly sensitive and dark poetry.

Many people with a minor John will also have some inner demons or a slight chip on their shoulder. This is the easiest way to spot someone's John minor sign. Your happy-go-lucky Ringo boss may have some sadness in her life she won't easily share. Or your down-to-earth vegan George boyfriend may also feel compelled to drink a little too much to drown his sorrows. This characteristic can also manifest itself as anger or negative energy. If you've ever seen your Paul friend explode in a rage when an old lady doesn't understand the concept of the fast lane, he's probably got a John minor.

A John minor can also manifest as impulsivity and bad decision-making. While Georges are known for being thoughtful, if they occasionally blow $500 on a bunch of piñatas for a birthday party, they might have a John rising. We've all seen that normally rational friend make a completely irrational choice. Chances are, they have a John minor.

If you have a John minor sign:

- You occasionally sulk.
- You are uncharacteristically pessimistic.
- Sometimes you are conceited.
- You're occasionally impulsive or make poor decisions.

Paul Minor

People with a Paul minor, no matter their major Beatle Sign, share several similar characteristics. Since Pauls are one of the stronger signs in Beatleology, individuals with Paul minors will also share the tendency to be domineering. For example, in the workplace, most Ringos are content to let others fight it out to be top banana. They don't need to be the loudest voice at meetings. However, the Ringo with a Paul rising will occasionally feel it necessary to assert his or her control (especially when other Pauls get too pushy).

Paul minor signs also give people a certain amount of positive energy and enthusiasm. Georges aren't usually known for being upbeat and manic. But a George with a Paul rising will have a tendency to be cheery, fun, and light. This George will occasionally exhibit a seemingly endless positive energy when others simply want to give up.

Those with a Paul minor sign are frequently narcissistic. One endearing quality of a Ringo is often lack of ego. But a Ringo with a Paul rising will definitely have an ego. And that ego will occasionally flare up, like during the company softball game. The other Ringos are content to let everyone bat and have a good time, but the one with the Paul rising will only care about *winning* and hitting a home run.

If you have a Paul minor sign:

- You tend to be popular at work and school.
- You are uncharacteristically giving.
- You might be pushy and demanding.
- You occasionally lack tact.

George Minor

Not surprisingly, many people have a George minor sign. Simply put, many people have a quiet, shy side to their personalities. The John who is quiet at parties or the Ringo who is reserved can often have a George minor. Ringos love people, but a Ringo with a George rising will often seek "alone time." Many individuals with a George minor can only take so much of being around others. For example, minor Georges will often spend Sundays reading, doing puzzles, or playing computer games to recharge their batteries for the work week.

George minors also make people more rational and practical. While most Ringos will think nothing of blowing a week's pay on margaritas and body shots at their local Señor Frog's, a Ringo with a George rising will think of paying his child support first.

Other people with a George minor are frequently passive-aggressive. Johns, for instance, are often upfront with their feelings of anger and conflict. When they possess a George minor, they might display their anger with more subtlety. For instance, this John with a George rising might get even with her coworker by tossing her salad out of the company refrigerator, thereby forcing her to buy something much more fattening (bitch).

If you have a George minor sign:

- You have a tendency to be spiritual.
- You have an uncharacteristic ability to be insightful and analytical (especially for Pauls and Ringos).
- You are occasionally withdrawn.

Ringo Minor

Those with a Ringo minor have an easygoing attitude and an ability to let things go. Georges and Johns can often be too uptight for their own good, but if they have a Ringo minor sign, they might have a completely different side. If your boss is a nose-to-the-grind kind of slave driver, but on the weekend she loves to go country line dancing, she might have a Ringo minor. Maybe your husband works overtime every day, but loves to cut loose by going to the game, tailgating, and painting his body in team colors. Either person may have a Ringo rising.

Another minor Ringo trait is the propensity toward popularity. Georges are usually not part of the cool kid crowd, but those with a Ringo minor can be. The Ringo aspect of their personality will help make them more endearing to their peers and cause them to seek out recognition.

Ringo minors can also be exceedingly shallow and vain. Usually Johns and Georges are fairly deep people both spiritually and intellectually. But those with a Ringo rising have the unfortunate tendency to be a little shallow. Most male Georges don't care much about fashion (if they are fashionable, it's only to fit in or as a societal requirement). However, if they have a Ringo minor, they are much more likely to spend a small fortune at Banana Republic or wax their chest.

People with this minor sign can often be a bit hedonistic. Ringo minors like to overindulge with food, drugs, or alcohol (or all three). A Paul with a Ringo rising might spend the week eating organic tofu salads and wheatgrass smoothies, but on Friday night he'll binge on a quart of mai tais and two orders of chili-cheese fries. Many people with a Ringo minor are frequently overweight.

If you have a Ringo minor sign:

- You are usually underappreciated.
- You have an uncharacteristic ability to be charming and pleasant.
- You might lust after the material possessions of others.

How a Minor Sign Develops Throughout Life

Unlike your major Beatle sign, which you are born with like DNA and fingerprints, your minor sign often develops during your childhood. Simply put, minor signs are environmental; they can change over the course of your life. Many factors go into shaping your minor sign, including your parents (whether or not they locked you in a closet) and your adolescent and early adult experiences. Just as twins raised by different families can create two very different adults, environment can make two extremely diverse Johns, Pauls, Georges, or Ringos.

Interestingly, minor signs can, on occasion, change during the course of a lifetime. One reason is a dramatic change in environment. For example, a New Yorker who suddenly moves to Sedona, Arizona, might slowly find his minor John morphing into a minor Paul. The second reason is occupational. Yes, your job can change your minor Beatle Sign.

Parents

As much as we hate to admit it, our parents have the greatest impact on who we are as individuals and how we perceive the world. During our childhood, they also have the most influence in shaping our minor Beatle Signs. As they teach us ethics, responsibility, or how to cut a brick of hashish, they are also helping us develop our rising sign.

For instance, Donald Trump's children will quickly learn to be egotistical and hedonistic, making their minors either Pauls or Ringos. Even if linguist Noam Chomsky's children are Ringos, they will have a tendency to have George minors. The examples go on and on.

The habits we learn in childhood we often take into adulthood. This is true for our minor signs as well. If your parents are more cerebral and enjoy reading, the arts, and visiting museums, your minor sign is more likely to be that of a George or John. If your parents loved to barbecue and drink copious amounts of light beer, you will have a good chance of becoming a Ringo minor.

Adolescent Experiences

Ah, adolescence—a time of joy and self discovery for some; a time of bitterness and pain for others. Whatever your experience, your adolescent period helped define who you are as a person and shaped your minor Beatle Sign.

People who experienced a more challenging adolescence by not fitting in or being bullied often develop John or George minor signs. Thirty years later, those who had a difficult time in their formative years may still have a chip on their shoulder and that can manifest itself in this way. Those who were considered popular, beautiful, and talented may develop a Paul or Ringo minor sign.

Minor Sign Changes Later in Life

The day-in, day-out aspect of the working environment has a major impact on personality. Being a "lifty" at a ski resort has a tendency to turn people into Ringo minors. Real estate agents all slowly become Paul minors whether they like it or not. Computer techs all develop a George minor. And middle-school teachers will soon produce a minor John. Luckily, retirement can often alter a minor sign by taking the individual out of a particular situation.

How does this happen? When we work with other people, there is a human tendency to mesh our personalities with those close to us. Since many of us spend forty hours a week at work, it's no coincidence that we begin to exhibit some different Beatle traits.

To be sure, these changes are slow, occurring over a period of years or decades. But they can happen. It's important for the Beatleologist to realize what is happening to his or her personality and watch for signs of change.

Occupations and Their Likely Minor Signs

Wall Street: Paul minor
Real estate: Paul minor
College professor: George minor
Teacher: John minor
Therapist/counselor: John minor
Retail: John minor
Priest/reverend/rabbi: George minor
Bartender: Ringo minor
Stripper: Ringo minor
Travel agent: Ringo minor
Veterinarian: George minor
Car sales: Paul minor
Engineering: John minor
Law: John minor
Mortician: John minor
Adult film star: Ringo minor
Politician: Paul minor
Nurse: John minor
Accountant: George minor
Police officer: John minor
Construction worker: Ringo minor
Pharmacist: Ringo minor
Dentist: George minor

The Real Fab Four's Minor Signs

Yes, it's true. The actual Beatles had their own minor signs. How can that be, you ask? Aren't they our cosmic models for Beatleology? Beatle Signs are based on the iconic aspects of their personalities. Like all people, they are complex individuals who had both their own major and minor signs. We will explore each Beatle's minor sign and how it affected their work, relationships, and destinies.

John Lennon with a Rising Ringo

Yes, John Lennon was a John with a Ringo rising. For many, that's a hard pill to swallow, but John exhibited many Ringo-like qualities during his lifetime, especially in his younger years. Many of us think of John as an intense genius with a very troubled side. He certainly had a chip on his shoulder after the abandonment by his father and his mother's untimely death. So, how could this troubled kid also have a Ringo minor sign?

In his teenage years, John was a notorious jokester. He was always up for a good laugh and a good prank at school. Instead of paying attention in class, he often drew satirical comics of the faculty. In fact, many of John's early friends and acquaintances never knew his serious side. They just witnessed his devil-may-care attitude. Like all Ringos, John was often flippant. Nevertheless, he was also popular (a strong Ringo trait), and the other Beatles looked up to him.

Also like most Ringos, John loved to have a good time. He enjoyed having a few pints at the local pub and getting pissed during his Liverpool days. Later on, he took amphetamines to keep up with a grueling performance schedule in Hamburg. Once the Beatles were introduced to marijuana and LSD, there was no going back for him.

Paul McCartney with a Rising John

Paul McCartney is definitely a Paul, but he also has a John as a minor sign. As we have seen, the two strongest signs in Beatleology share many traits. Deep down, and off camera, Paul could often think and act like John. How could this happy, cute Beatle have a troubled dark side?

First, Paul had a tendency to be rather pushy, especially when it came to the Beatles' music. This was particularly true with Stuart Sutcliffe and later George Harrison. During the Beatles' early years, Paul resented Stu's place in the band despite his lack of ability (and his place in John's heart). Paul quietly worked on Stu until he quit. During the Beatles' recording career, Paul often pushed George Harrison around, demanding that he play a certain way.

Like a John, Paul McCartney has made some not-so-wise decisions about women. While his relationship with Linda seems straight from a storybook, his marriage to Heather Mills reads like something out of a Stephen King novel. Like other Johns, Paul McCartney was searching for that love in his life, maybe a replacement for his long-lost mother.

George Harrison with a Rising Paul

While it might cause George Harrison to turn over in his grave, it's true that his minor sign was a Paul. It's well known that the two didn't get along well, especially in the later years of the Beatles. But there is definitely a part of Paul in George Harrison.

Most of George Harrison's Paul traits relate to ego. While George is often viewed as the quiet, humble Beatle, beneath the surface he had an ego the size of Yankee Stadium. This trait is true of many

Georges with Pauls rising; they'll never admit it, but they think they are pretty damn good at what they do.

George Harrison could also be stubborn. Just like a Paul, he wanted things done his way. True, he wasn't as vocal about it as the other Beatles, but George had a vision for every song he wrote (and felt they were just as good as the Lennon/McCartney offerings).

Ringo Starr with a Rising George

As hard as it is to believe, Ringo Starr's minor sign is a George. How can the fun-loving, outgoing Ringo Starr also have characteristics of a George, you ask? He's the last person you would expect to be slightly withdrawn or introverted. But it's true. He's also a George rising.

First and foremost, Ringo's George-like qualities are related to the fact that he never gets credit for anything the Beatles accomplished. Ringo is haunted by the old "I'm just happy to be here" aspect of his association with the group. In truth, Ringo is a talented musician. Like many Georges, Ringo never received credit for being a competent musician and songwriter. He wrote hits such as "Octopus's Garden" and played central roles in the films, *A Hard Day's Night* and *Help!* because he was arguably the best actor. Additionally, Ringo never gets credit for his contributions to drumming and percussion. In fact, while the other Beatles were still learning their craft in Hamburg and Liverpool, Ringo was already a professional (and highly sought after) drummer. It was only after the Beatles first signed a record deal with George Martin and Parlophone that he considered joining the group.

Ringo's other George-esque traits lie in his ability to defer to others. Georges are often the least pushy person in the room and this was definitely true of Ringo Starr. When Ringo tried to present original material to the other members of the band, they often shunned it or claimed it sounded like another commercial hit. Ringo, with his George minor sign, tended not to push any farther. Sadly, Ringo wasn't confident enough with himself or his music to make more of a contribution to the albums.

Famous Minor Signs

While history and world events are shaped by individuals and their Beatle signs, the role of minor signs cannot be ignored. Like the rest of us, celebrities and historical figures often have minor signs that affect their actions, beliefs, and social interactions. Former president Bill Clinton is a classic Paul with seemingly boundless energy and enthusiasm. He is well liked, and yet he is a strong advocate for his own agenda. He can be pushy and dominating when necessary. Interestingly, his minor sign is a Ringo with his tendency toward hedonism and a love of buxom women and fatty food. Clinton also likes to cut loose and have a good time by playing his saxophone or devouring a few Big Macs (until his recent Mac Attack, that is).

Moses is a classic John due to his stubborn idealism and concern for social and political justice. Moses' minor sign would most likely be a Paul manifesting itself at his rage with his people for worshiping the golden calf in his absence. Pauls have a "my way or the highway" point of view and can't stand things going on without them.

Kurt Vonnegut's understated charm and social commentary make him an obvious George. However, he also had a flippant, comical side and didn't take life too seriously, making his minor sign a Ringo.

In many ways, Bob Dylan is a classic John. He's artistic, he's a little troubled, and he was often misunderstood during his prime. However, Dylan also exhibits many traits of a George. Dylan's George rising often manifested itself as shyness and introversion. He was notoriously tight-lipped around the press. When ungrateful fans became too much for him, Dylan turned inward and took a long break from the music industry.

Abraham Lincoln's George-esque traits are well known. Lincoln was an archetypal George; he was thoughtful, introverted, and pragmatic. But most aren't aware that Lincoln had a John rising. On a personal level, Lincoln was quite troubled. He was haunted by the death of his sons. Like a John, Lincoln could also go overboard in order to push his agenda, as seen in his suspension of civil liberties during the Civil War.

Martin Luther King Jr. was a Paul with a George rising. Like a Paul, Dr. King believed deeply in his work and pushed himself to succeed. The civil rights activist was also a born leader, a trait often seen in Pauls. But he also had a quieter, more philosophical side, making his minor sign a George. As a Christian minister, Dr. King was obviously highly conscious of his own spirituality and those of others. He had an inner peace often characteristic of Georges. Before his assassination, he went so far as to say it didn't matter if he lived, he was at peace with the Lord and the world.

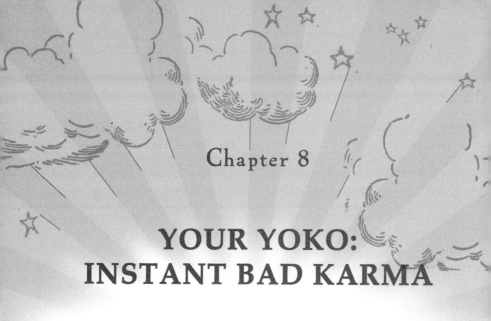

Chapter 8

YOUR YOKO: INSTANT BAD KARMA

Is there someone in your life who:

- Brings you down?

- Often talks you into making poor decisions?

- Brings out your worst qualities?

- Gets you into trouble?

- Causes you to spend frivolously?

- Helps to alienate you from your friends and family?

In Beatleology, that person is known as your Yoko.

Much has been made of Yoko Ono's influence on John and her contribution to the breakup of the Beatles. In Beatle mythology, she is often cited as ruining John both artistically and spiritually. Beatleology borrows from this legend to create the concept of a Yoko. While Yoko is not considered a major sign in Beatleology, she nonetheless has an important role in Beatleology.

Your Yoko is defined as someone who brings you down, who steers you in a self-destructive direction, who pushes you toward your dark side and nurtures your base instincts. Your Yoko can be anyone, and often changes throughout the course of your life. For example, in fifth grade, Billy Jenkins, the class clown, encouraged you to act inappropriately and ignore your social studies work. He was your Yoko. In high school, it would have never occurred to you to skip third period and take a bong rip in the parking lot if it weren't for your Yoko. And you would have probably finished college if your Yoko boyfriend hadn't bought cheap condoms, and now, just like John, you have a Yoko spouse.

Identifying your Yoko is not always easy. It requires discipline and self-reflection. Ask yourself, "Who is currently bringing me down and pushing me in the wrong direction? Yet, I'm strangely drawn to this person." If not carefully identified, your Yoko can ruin your life. No matter what your sign in Beatleology, a Yoko can be a destructive force. Yokos are unique from person to person. My Yoko will not be the same as yours. In fact, you may be a Yoko yourself.

Identifying your Yoko is often difficult because, subconsciously, you don't want to admit this particular person is destroying your life. Just like an alcoholic doesn't want to admit he has a problem with booze, many of us don't want to admit we have a problem with our Yoko. This is partly why people stay in bad or abusive relationships. It is hard to recognize that a loved one is, in fact, hurting you. When trying to find your Yoko, it is best to close the door on denial.

One central tenet of Beatleology is to quickly identify your Yoko and minimize his or her negative influence on your life. Simply recognizing your Yoko and eliminating him or her from your life is not enough. If, for example, you divorce your Yoko husband and move to Poughkeepsie, your troubles are not over. A new Yoko will appear. Just as God must always have Satan, a Yoko will always exist in your life. It's not your Yoko's relationship to you; it's your relationship to your Yoko.

Yoko Ono's Life

Yoko Ono was born in Tokyo in 1933 to an aristocratic family who made their fortune in the Japanese banking industry. She attended the finest private schools, reserved only for the ruling class. At the onset of World War II, her family waited out the chaos and violence in the posh mountain resort of Karuizawa where the younger members of the Imperial family were also sent. After the war, Yoko's family returned to a relative state of normalcy.

Yoko became the first woman accepted into the prestigious philosophy program at Gakushuin University, but dropped out after two semesters. Yoko then moved with her family to just outside New York City where she attended Sarah Lawrence College. It was there that Yoko Ono was introduced to the burgeoning Bohemian, post-Dada, and avant-garde art movements. Inspired to create her own art, Yoko rented a loft and began conducting a series of performance art "pieces." In one of the first pieces, she nearly burned down the building by setting a painting on fire.

In 1956 she married composer Toshi Ichiyanagi, divorcing him six years later. Following the divorce, Yoko was sent to a mental institution in Japan after a suicide attempt. While recovering from her breakdown, musician, film producer, and art promoter Tony Cox flew to her bedside from New York. The two were married a short time later, but their hasty marriage did not work out. Tony and Yoko were soon witnessed threatening each other with kitchen knives. Unfortunately, during the course of all the drama between Yoko and Tony, a child was quickly conceived. In 1963, Yoko gave birth to Kyoko Chan Cox.

It was during this period that Yoko began experimenting with more performance art.

These interactive art pieces included *Cut Piece*, where audience members took turns cutting off pieces of Yoko's clothing, and *Touch Piece*, which consisted of nothing more than Yoko forcing audience members to touch their neighbor for over eight hours. The experimental film *No. 4* consisted solely of closeups of human buttocks. In *Stone Piece*, Yoko crawled into a large cloth bag and remained for hours.

Yoko's first meeting with John Lennon proved to be memorable and foreshadowed some of the stranger aspects of their relationship. In 1966, when the two met at a London art gallery, she handed him a note that read simply "Breathe." John instantly found this strange performance artist fascinating and challenging. Yoko Ono set about to place herself squarely into John's life, effectively destroying John's marriage to Cynthia Lennon. However, the two did not divorce for two more years.

From that point on, Yoko practically chained herself to Lennon. This inseparability caused great friction amongst the Beatles during the recording of *The White Album* and *Abbey Road*. Wives and girl-friends had never been allowed in the band's recording sessions. Yoko not only insisted on being present but would give criticism and even demand to participate. She constantly reinforced John's idea that the band's music was infantile and artistically dead. This was only exacerbated by the fact that John and Yoko had begun using heroin, along with dropping acid and smoking copious amounts of marijuana on a daily basis. Tensions in the band went from bad to worse, and disagreements about musical direction, as well as squabbles over the handling of their business dealings finally broke up the Beatles in 1970.

After the Beatles, Yoko had John all to herself. The two embarked on numerous artistic, political, notoriety-seeking endeavors. Fatefully, on December 8, 1980, John was shot to death by Mark David Chapman when he and Yoko were returning to their apartment in New York City. Chapman reportedly had hours of Beatles recordings and a copy of *Catcher in the Rye* in his pocket.

After Lennon's death, Yoko continued to promote her late husband's musical and artistic legacy.

Identifying Your Yoko

Everyone's Yoko is different and specific to the individual. Identifying him or her is key to a more Fab existence. To identify your Yoko, you should ask yourself, "Who is bringing me down? Who is nurturing my self-destructive side?" Also, "What could I achieve without this person's influence?" With these questions, you can begin to identify and minimize your Yoko. Think about yourself when you are at your worst, when you are acting most self-destructively. Who are you often with in these situations? Who is pushing you in this direction? These ideas are central to finding your Yoko.

Some Yokos will be obvious, while others will be extremely difficult to identify. This deceptive nature and ability to go undetected makes the Yoko's influence even more damaging. Your Yoko is very rarely your worst enemy. By defining someone as an enemy, you have already taken steps to counteract their menace. Much more often, a Yoko will manifest in the form of a friend or a loved one, which can make their influence much more damaging.

For example, Larry owns a health food store in a prosperous part of town. His business is thriving until Barry opens one across the street. Whenever Larry sends out a mailer (soy ink on hemp paper) advertising his big sale on fish oil and wheat germ smoothies, Barry counters with an ad featuring the same items at even lower prices. At first glance it would appear that Barry is Larry's Yoko. However his real Yoko is, in fact, Harry, his long-time employee who has been tipping off the competition in exchange for bootleg Allman Brothers CDs. The most destructive thing about a Yoko is the fact that he or she is usually someone close to you whom you trust.

How to Identify Your Yoko

Since Yokos take many different forms, identifying them isn't always easy. Your particular Yoko may only hinder part of your life. For instance, many Yokos affect your career, but some may just encumber your personal life. Use these questions to help discover your Yoko. Often this is a difficult task because our psyche does not want to admit that this person is hindering us. We are in denial about this person's negative impact on our life and subconsciously choose not to think about it.

- Who claims to be my best friend even though I haven't known him that long?
- What are my greatest assets in life, and what would this person have to gain by their loss?
- Who pulls me in directions I may not want to go and makes it seem like my idea?
- What are my weaknesses and who is secretly nurturing them?
- Who causes me to spend frivolously?
- Does someone want me all to herself?
- Who is the one person who, if he betrayed me, could destroy everything I hold dear?
- Am I being steered in directions that negatively affect my career?
- Is there a reason all of my other friends hate [fill in the blank]?
- Who do I depend on the most and what is her secret agenda?
- Is someone pulling me away from trusted friends and beloved family?
- Who is always with me when I'm at my worst?
- Who would benefit from my downfall?
- Who causes me to act self-destructively?
- Does someone use sex and love to manipulate me?
- Why is this person so nice to me?
- Do I act differently when I'm around this person?
- Is there someone who pushes me toward excess?
- Have I been asked to hold a press conference in which this person and myself sing from inside a large white sack and call the process "total communication" (John and Yoko, 1969)?

Dealing with Your Yoko

Quick Tips for Dealing with Your Yoko

Limit your Yoko's access.
Suggest alternative, nondestructive activities.
Limit your Yoko's control over your money.
Take a moment and think about the impact of what your
Yoko is asking of you.
Minimize the amount of time you spend together.
Change jobs or departments to avoid your Yoko.
Make sure other people are around when interacting with
your Yoko.
Take your Yoko out of his or her element.
Run away. Run away quickly.

There is no one correct method for dealing with your Yoko. In some cases, simply distancing yourself from the person may be enough. In other cases, this may not be possible and a calculated effort to minimize the Yoko's damage becomes more appropriate. In the most extreme cases, the only solution is to immediately drop everything and flee. How you deal with your Yoko will depend on the nature of your specific circumstance, but it will also depend on your Beatle Sign and the sign of your Yoko.

Distancing Yourself from Your Yoko

Often people find it impossible to completely eliminate their Yoko from their lives. This is the case when the Yoko happens to be a family member. If you realize your shopaholic sister who helped you rack up $15,000 in credit card debt is your Yoko, it's nearly impossible to cut all ties with her. You will see her at family functions and she will wonder why you never call. How do you deal with this Yoko? Again, keeping your Yoko at a controllable distance is key to diminishing her negative effect. For instance, if she suggests a trip to Rodeo Drive for a little shopping and lunch, you should suggest going on a hike. In the forest, it is nearly impossible to buy a $600 pair of shoes. By neutralizing your Yoko's negative effects on you, it's easy to keep her in check.

When you need to limit contact with a Yoko family member, you may need to make it a point to only see this relative at Christmas, Ramadan, and bar mitzvahs. While it may hurt his feelings, keeping your distance from your Yoko is essential to leading a happy, productive life.

If your Yoko is a coworker, distance is critical to maintaining a happy and successful workplace. Easier tricks include asking human resources to move your cubicle or requesting a different shift. Without hurting her feelings, you may need to transfer departments. And if things are really bad, you may need to transfer to another state altogether.

With Yoko family members, distance is important to keep in mind at all times. If your dead-beat Yoko brother asks to be your roommate, it's probably a good idea to keep this aspect of your lives separate. Also, you should take every effort to avoid becoming financially intertwined with a Yoko relative.

Minimizing Your Yoko's Effect

After becoming a Beatleologist, many people realize their Yoko is, in fact, a spouse, coworker, or good friend. This makes distancing yourself from your Yoko nearly impossible. Therefore, it's important to learn how to minimize your Yoko's negative effect on your life. The first key to minimization involves finding how your Yoko brings you down. A Yoko coworker will most likely affect your career. You may deal with this Yoko by limiting your contact during the day. It is just not feasible for most people to quit your job to avoid a Yoko. And remember, if you eliminate your Yoko, another will appear in his or her place.

When trying to reduce the impact of your Yoko, you need to learn to step back for a moment and think about how the person brings you down. After considering this, it's often in your best interest to act in the opposite manner. Remember, a Yoko feeds your id, your base instincts. If you consciously act against this impulse, it soon becomes easy to minimize his or her effect.

Now, why shouldn't you get a divorce if you realize your Yoko is your spouse? To be honest, in certain cases you *should* get divorced. However, many times, it isn't necessary. If there are children involved, it's not easy just to end the marriage. Also, sometimes your Yoko only affects one aspect of your life. For example, your husband may be very supportive of your career but is your Yoko when it comes to your expensive wine addiction. Therefore, learning how to minimize his impact is essential to achieving happiness.

When to Run from Your Yoko

Discovering your Yoko can often be a highly disturbing event. You may have never guessed it was someone you loved so much or held so close. It may be a girlfriend, a boss, a family member, or any number of people. In extreme cases, you will realize your Yoko is negatively affecting many aspects of your life. It's one thing if your

Yoko only affects your career. It's another if he or she has a harmful impact on your career, family, love life, and finances. This is the scariest Yoko of all. This is the Yoko they taught you to stop, drop, and roll away from.

Obviously, there are only certain Yokos you can completely eliminate from your life. Bosses, girlfriends, boyfriends, and friends top the list. As painful as it may be, sometimes you must cut all ties to this person. If your girlfriend is making your life miserable, spending all of your money, and causing you all sorts of grief, you need to dump her. Besides, all of your friends probably hate her anyway. Yoko bosses are especially tough, but you may need to consider a career move.

Your Cynthia

Cynthia Lennon, John Lennon's first wife, stood by her husband through thick and thin, enduring a lot of pain as a result. Even when they were first dating and John was away with the band in Hamburg, he relentlessly cheated on her. Despite this, she always welcomed him home with open arms. Later, as the Beatles' careers took off, she was forced to keep their marriage a secret and had to care for John's baby alone in a squalid apartment. Over the years, she endured John's countless affairs and increasingly erratic behavior until she was finally pushed aside for Yoko Ono.

In Beatleology, the opposite of your Yoko is your Cynthia. Your Cynthia is your ultimate supporter who will stick by you no matter what, even to the point of taking abuse. Your Cynthia is often your mom or a grandparent. They are the one who will always visit you in prison. Ironically, you are often your Cynthia's Yoko.

For example, Abraham Lincoln was Mary Todd Lincoln's Cynthia and John Lennon was Cynthia's Yoko. While Lincoln supported his wife, she ran around Washington racking up debt in uncontrollable spending sprees. Her actions almost derailed the man who was arguably the greatest American president. One key to happiness in the Beatle-verse is to embrace your supportive Cynthia while distancing yourself from your Yoko who will inevitably bring you down. Also, try not to be your Cynthia's Yoko. After all, your Cynthia is there to help you. It is possible for you to be your Cynthia's Cynthia and this is a very desirable state of equi-Beatle-librium. The "Cynthia vs. Yoko" conundrum is a question as old as humanity itself. Your Cynthia is very understanding, stable, and supportive but unglamorous and sometimes boring. Your Yoko is exciting, challenging, and seductive, but he or she can also bring you to your knees and ultimately destroy you. Why do men sometimes leave their loving wives and families and run off to Costa Rica with a bipolar stripper who ends up selling their kidneys? Why do women sometimes shoot down all of the stable, employed, polite men who ask them out in favor of dating unemployed, violent, hard-drinking tattoo enthusiasts who steal their money, knock them up, and sleep with their sisters? The answer is clear: the classic "Cynthia vs. Yoko" paradox.

Why You Will Never Be Totally Yoko-Free

Unfortunately, your life will never be completely Yoko-less. Beatleology borrows the concept of the Yoko from Buddhism in the idea that life is suffering and all we can do is try to minimize its effect on us. If you run away from one Yoko, another will arise.

This is not to say that some Yokos should not be eliminated from your life. You should immediately separate from an abusive love, unless they are very wealthy. You should quit any job where the boss makes your life miserable, but be sure you're not leaving for an even worse employment situation. There will always be a Yoko in your life, but the important thing is how you deal with the relationship.

Famous People and Their Yokos

Julius Caesar

Caesar's murder by his close friend Brutus is another classic example of a Yoko from the ancient world. Like many Yokos, Brutus was a trusted confidant of Caesar, which prompted Caesar to ask, "Et tu, Brute?" upon being stabbed by his onetime friend.

King Louis XVI

King Louis XVI of France's Yoko was his wife Marie Antoinette. She was a wildly unpopular queen at the time leading up to the French Revolution. She was known for being a vacuous party girl. While scholars agree she didn't say, "Let them eat cake," it was true she was completely out of touch with the common people of France. She only made Louis even less popular and helped bring about his end on the guillotine.

Sid Vicious

Sid Vicious of the legendary punk band, the Sex Pistols, lived fast and died young thanks to his Yoko, Nancy Spungen. While Sid lacked musical talent, he projected a great image for the Sex Pistols.

Unfortunately, Sid met Nancy in London in 1977. She was already a heroin addict and quickly got Sid hooked as well. Much like John and Yoko, the two had a drug-fueled, manic relationship that helped bring an end to the band. Nancy then became his "manager," which basically meant sitting around the Chelsea Hotel in New York and getting wasted on smack. Things there got so bad that Nancy was eventually murdered, likely by Sid's own hand. His heroin addiction soon proved to spell his end. Brought down by his Yoko, Vicious overdosed in February 1979.

George W. Bush

Sometimes your Yoko is your must trusted confidant and advisor. They are also known for pushing their way into your life. This couldn't be truer of George W. Bush's Yoko, Dick Cheney. Cheney infamously forced his way into the vice presidency (he was head of the vice-presidential selection committee and picked himself). Once in office, Dick championed the idea of the Iraq war despite lack of evidence for WMDs. He also convinced W. to abandon several constitutional rights with items like the Patriot Act and using Guantanamo Bay as a prison for suspected terrorists. Had Bush recognized Cheney as his Yoko and followed a more centrist agenda, the legacy of his presidency might be very different today.

Mel Gibson

What could bring down one of the most successful actors/directors/producers of all time? How about a vicious anti-Semitic tirade during a drunk-driving arrest? (How did the subject of Zionist domination conspiracy theories even come up in the conversation? "Can I see your license, registration, and dreidel, please?") Mel learned his particular blend of racial, religious, and political beliefs from his Yoko, his father Hutton Gibson, who was an outspoken fundamentalist Christian and anti-Semite. G'day, mate!

Michael Vick

Former Falcons quarterback Michael Vick was once considered the luckiest athlete on the planet. He had a top NFL contract and endorsement deals with Coke, Nike, and Powerade. Everything came crashing down when Vick decided to involve himself with violent dogfights and the Bad Newz Kennel. Michael's Yoko was Quanis Phillips, a childhood friend who drew Vick into the world of illegal dogfights at an early age. This is a perfect example of how a Yoko can ruin your life, finances, and reputation.

Barry Bonds, Gary Sheffield, and Jason Giambi

Sluggers Barry Bonds, Gary Sheffield, and Jason Giambi share the same Yoko. Convicted felon Greg Anderson is a former personal trainer who allegedly provided Bonds with steroids. Through Bonds, Sheffield and Giambi also became involved with the illicit juice. Even though these three were already mega-stars, their Yoko stroked their egos, pushing them over the edge. Your Yoko is known for destroying your reputation and encouraging your self-destructive side.

Chapter 9

BEATLE LOVE:
ALL YOU NEED IS LOVE

The Beatles wrote some of the most memorable love songs of the twentieth century. For many, the Beatles were the essence of sexuality and love. Whether it was a first crush or a first kiss, the Beatles' music often stirs up old memories and feelings. Before the Baby Boomer generation could experience "free love," they had to learn to "hold your hand."

Like all other aspects of life, your Beatle Sign determines your view of love and approach to romance. Each Beatle sees love, relationships, and sex very differently—and when those views collide, you get a unique outcome.

Beatle Signs also determine one's compatibility with his or her lover's Inner Beatle. A couple's relationship is governed by how their individual Beatles interact. For instance, a George lover will have a completely different reaction in a relationship with a Paul than with a John. If she's with another George, that relationship will be different still. As you can see, these diverse combinations are practically endless (okay, just ten).

This chapter will help you explore how your Inner Beatle approaches love and relationships with other Beatles.

Beatle Sign Pairings in Love

The following descriptions will provide you with a clear indication of the positives and negatives of all the Beatle love pairings. Love is mysterious, but sometimes we should know what we're getting into.

Johns and Johns

A John paired with a John tends to be:

- Codependent
- Isolating
- Egalitarian
- Loving

Johns are intense, devoted, and occasionally psychotic lovers. They often pick mates who encourage their darker side and bad behaviors. Two Johns in a relationship or marriage can magnify this effect exponentially. So it's important for two Johns to be aware of this tendency if they have any hope of making their relationship work. Two Johns will quickly put their romance in the forefront of their lives at the neglect of their professions and friends. Together, they can block out others and isolate themselves in a world they see as romantic bliss (which makes the rest of us gag). For their relationship to remain healthy, they must make the conscious effort to hang out with friends, have time apart, and cultivate hobbies. They need to avoid constant e-mails, phone calls, and text messages. To be precise, they need to take it easy.

Two Johns have a nasty tendency of encouraging each other's bad habits. If your John boyfriend smokes the occasional joint before work, you may quickly find yourself sucked into his routine if you're not careful. Or if he wants to rob a liquor store to pay off your loans, you may be tempted to join him. Ultimately, it's important for two Johns to try to avoid dragging each other down. Remember, Johns are very skilled at making bad ideas seem brilliant.

If two Johns must have a relationship (e.g., no one was able to convince them otherwise), it is critical they create certain boundaries and make time for themselves and other friends. They should avoid isolating their relationship from the outside world. All guys have had a buddy who, once in a relationship, stopped hanging out, and started to spend his free time shopping at Pottery Barn. Most likely it was a John/John combination. Two Johns must also realize that every night does not have to be a date. Sometimes a Tuesday night is just a Tuesday night. It can't all be magical.

On the upside, two Johns will have a very egalitarian relationship. Neither partner will dominate the other and traditional gender roles will be thrown out the window. A male John won't demand dinner, and a female John wouldn't even think of doing the dishes every night. Both will feel responsible for their love, home, and children. It is rare that this pair will have a traditional marriage. More likely, two Johns will create a home based around the idea of a partnership and making life better together.

Two Johns will also have a very loving relationship. Emotions will be expressed both verbally and physically. These two signs together will rarely experience intimacy issues.

Johns and Pauls

A John paired with a Paul tends to be:

- Intense
- Codependent
- Committed
- Turbulent
- Toxic
- Creative
- Magical

Johns and Pauls are the most dominant signs in Beatleology. They are the light and dark. So it follows that a relationship between a John and Paul is a mix of good and bad, lightness and darkness. These two signs definitely make for an intense marriage or partnership. It can be magical and it can be toxic; sometimes both.

Johns and Pauls are known for jumping into a relationship with both feet. Often when these two signs begin dating (to the dismay of friends), they have the propensity to move the relationship along quickly. If you've ever had a buddy who met some girl at a party on Friday and moved into her apartment by Monday, they could be a John-Paul pair. This couple should also beware of their proclivity for codependence. It's important to have space. Unlike a John-John relationship, however, a Paul will feel more of a need to keep his or her friendships intact. For a John and Paul romance to work, they first need to take their time in love. It is critical for both partners to get to know each other. They should avoid the desire to smother. Even if you want to break into her house and cover her bed with rose petals, you must remember that idea can always wait until the third date. Additionally, each sign should make a conscious effort to keep other friendships and have some "me" time. Johns, especially, should avoid their propensity for overdramatization. Remember, if your Paul wife doesn't call you from the grocery store, it doesn't mean she doesn't love you.

Many John and Paul relationships can start out strong but burn out over time. Both signs continually seek love and affirmation. So, initially, the two will meet each other's emotional needs with lots of hugs, hand holding, flowers, and love poems. But after time, these relationships often become strained. They each tend to resent the other's dominance and emotional demands. Soon, this couple will start to play games with the other's feelings. When a John and Paul pair begin withholding affection and sex, it's time to move on.

Johns and Georges
A John paired with a George tends to be:

151

- Loving
- Withdrawn
- Stable
- Uncommunicative

A John and George relationship often has a very good chance of success. The positive traits of each sign complement the other, and their negative traits can cancel each other out. For instance, a hot-headed John can be balanced by a calm, level-headed George. So while the John boyfriend may want to pick a fight in a bar, the George girlfriend will tell him it's not worth it. Inversely, a John's need for love and companionship can negate a George's tendency to be distant and aloof. Since Georges often have a minimal number of bad habits, they can help Johns avoid being so damn self-destructive all the time.

A John and George marriage or relationship can be loving. Both partners may have a little trouble expressing their feelings, but the love will be felt. Luckily, their expressions of love won't be stifling or scary. It's highly unlikely a George will jump out of a giant cake, buck-naked, during your board of directors meeting. The John in the relationship is much more likely to feel unloved by the George. It's critical that the Johns ask the Georges about their feelings or understand they have a hard time expressing their emotions.

These two signs make for a stable relationship. It is doubtful the George in the romance will make any sudden moves or say things he or she will regret. However, these two signs also have the tendency to be uncommunicative. When frustrated or angered, both can emotionally shut down and shun other people. This couple must make it a point to talk about problems or it can boil over into a great big pot of resentment.

Johns and Ringos

A John paired with a Ringo tends to be:

- Intense
- Short-lived
- Easygoing
- Unfaithful

Johns and Ringos make for an excellent romantic pairing. Since Ringos have a pragmatic approach to romance, this can often offset a John's more intense and smothering ways. Ringos also have realistic expectations of their lovers. So, if their John isn't perfect, the relationship can still be successful (this is especially true of female Ringos and male Johns). Ringos will often act as the rock in the relationship and keep their John partner more centered. A thoughtful John will appreciate his partner's ability to keep him grounded. For the John, a Ringo makes an excellent domestic partner who prefers to have a home. Johns are more of a wandering soul but occasionally need to return to that nest. A sense of domestic tranquility is very good for a John.

A John and a Ringo are also likely to fall into a short but intense fling. Both Beatle Signs enjoy sex and love the sense of affirmation it brings. These two signs will often get together in extramarital affairs, but this is not to say these two signs can't work in a marriage or long-term partnership. The John, especially, must work to meet the Ringo's needs and appreciate all he or she does.

Unfortunately, John and Ringo relationships often have a short shelf life. Both Johns and Ringos need to be aware of their propensity toward infidelity. If their relationship becomes stale or strained, both signs have few qualms looking elsewhere for love. Both signs tend to gravitate toward short-term fulfillment at the expense of their relationships.

Ringos and Johns both have a tendency to overdo and enjoy life a little too much. This couple should be wary that their weekly wine tasting doesn't turn into a nightly wine binge. It is important for each partner to keep the other in check.

Pauls and Pauls

A Paul paired with a Paul tends to be:

- Codependent
- Obnoxious
- Intense
- Smothering
- Loving

Pauls are very loving and caring individuals. They seek out romantic love and security. They also need constant reassurance and affirmation of their love. This is why, under the right circumstances, two Pauls can work well in love. Under the wrong circumstances, they can be an utter disaster.

When two Pauls work well together in romance, they are being consistent partners, constantly reinforcing their love with cute notes, phone calls, and hugs. It is important for both Pauls to feel that daily affirmation. Pauls require a sense of security in their relationships, even after thirty years of marriage.

Two Pauls will also stroke each other's delicate ego. A Paul needs someone to tell her that her poetry and Thomas Kinkade–inspired paintings are beautiful. And who better to do that than another Paul. For the Paul couples, it is important to remember to take time to appreciate the other person's projects and activities. If there is a balance between the two Pauls, both taking turns at center stage, the couple can last a long time.

If left unchecked, two Pauls can create a very unhealthy, codependent relationship. Each person will feed off the other, feeling the need to stay in constant contact. Also, the two Pauls may get involved in one-upping each other ("I love you," "No, I love you," "No, I love you more."). Therefore, it's important for this pairing to establish boundaries. One phone call during the workday will suffice. Pauls must also make an effort to keep up other relationships and participate in activities that don't involve their partner. It is important for Pauls to set aside nights for other friends or sports.

Pauls can also be selfish and pig-headed. One partner can often grow to resent the other Paul's egocentric actions. Two Pauls often complain that the other dictates all activities in the relationship. It's critical for Pauls to let their other partner occasionally pick the movie or vacation spot.

While not overly sexual, Pauls are a highly loving and affectionate sign. They need constant physical contact and love. It's not rare to see two Pauls holding hands or embracing, or making out in public like a couple of teenagers. Pauls should not withhold affection during a quarrel as it only serves to extend the injury.

Pauls and Georges

A Paul paired with a George tends to be:

- Resentful
- Unaffectionate
- Short-lived

Arguably, Pauls and Georges make the worst romantic pairing in all of Beatleology. Without sounding too much like your mother, these two signs should not get together. Only bad things can happen. Why, you ask? As we've seen, Pauls and Georges are the two most antagonistic signs in Beatle Science. They are complete opposites. True, opposites can sometimes attract, but not these two.

To start with, since Georges are a more passive sign, they will quickly grow to resent a Paul's strong will and dominance in the relationship. Pauls like to assert themselves and will instinctually become the "leader" of the relationship. This can manifest itself in many ways, from always picking the restaurant, to choosing dating activities, to decisions about the relationship itself. Simply put, Pauls want their way. It's not that Georges don't, but they won't be as pushy about it as a Paul. They hate the way Pauls always seem to elbow their way to the front of everything. But when faced with a Paul, Georges can often step back and let it all happen, secretly growing resentful and angry. If a George and a Paul find themselves in a relationship, the Paul must make it a point to give his or her George partner a voice. Also, the George must strive to assert his or her feelings and wishes if the relationship has any chance of working.

"Why are you so distant? Don't you love me?"

"You're always smothering me. I need my personal space."

Does this conversation sound familiar? It's just an example of a classic Paul-George love conflict. Another reason this pairing is often troubled is that a Paul frequently smothers his or her partner. Georges like their space and time alone, whereas Pauls need constant contact, interaction, and affirmation. These two conflicting needs can spell trouble in a romance. A female Paul will especially find her George boyfriend distant and say things like "Sometimes I think he just doesn't care." This Paul needs to learn that a George won't express his love and affection as she might. Her George boyfriend ought to learn to not be so freaked out by all of the homemade cards with hearts drawn all over them. That's just who a Paul is.

Paul and George relationships are often short-lived. Once each sign learns more about the other's behaviors and tendencies, resentment quickly sets in. For example, at first a George may appreciate the affection and sweet gestures of his Paul girlfriend. But soon he will grow tired of the constant attention. The Paul will feel the George is too distant and withdrawn. At this point, the relationship often falls apart.

So, what if you just discovered you're in a Paul-George marriage with two kids and you don't live in a no-fault divorce state? What do you do now? Obviously, there have been successful Paul-George relationships. But how did they make them work? First, they learned to acknowledge each other's general inclinations in life. They learned to spot and respect the other's common behaviors and attitudes. The George must learn to be assertive and to reciprocate some of their partner's affection. The Paul needs to learn to let go of the reins once in a while and give their George some space. Only then does this pairing have a chance at success.

Pauls and Ringos

A Paul paired with a Ringo tends to be:

- Loving
- Highly sexual
- Uncomplicated

Ringos have an innate ability to connect with all of the signs in Beatleology. This is no truer than in love. Fittingly, Pauls and Ringos can make for great romantic couples and fulfilling marriages.

First and foremost, Pauls and Ringos love to feel loved. They both have a strong need to feel treasured by others, and luckily, they tend to fulfill this need in each other. A Paul may be more overt with his or her feelings, but Ringos don't have any problem reciprocating. Many Ringos carry a sense that they were unloved or underappreciated as children. Their Paul partner often meets that need for affirmation. For their part, Pauls need constant reminders of love. While their Ringo lover may not write them haiku poetry every day of the week, they like to express their adoration in simple ways like hugs, kisses, and, of course, sex.

A Ringo-Paul relationship is often highly sexual. This is mainly the influence of the Ringo. Pauls are not overly sexual; they use sex as a sort of confirmation of their partner's love. They willingly participate in sex because they need to feel accepted. To them, sex is often a means of getting to the snuggling that immediately follows. Luckily, these needs of the two signs complement each other. The Ringo, especially if he's the male in the relationship, should not take advantage of the Paul's willingness to comply sexually. And the Paul should never withhold sex as a way of maintaining power in the relationship.

In heterosexual relationships, Paul-Ringo relationships work best if the male partner is the Ringo. He will appreciate having an attractive partner who adores him. The male Ringo will also welcome the fact his Paul girlfriend will use sex as a way to confirm their relationship (i.e., he will get laid more). She will like his easygoing attitude and ability to go with *her* flow.

Pauls and Ringos enjoy uncomplicated relationships and romances. The Ringo's easygoing attitude often helps balance out the more intense Paul. And the Ringo will have the ability to shrug off some of the Paul's more domineering ways.

Both Pauls and Ringos have a strong desire to nest. Family is important to both of these signs. Despite his success as a rock star, Ringo Starr enjoyed being at home with his family, serving the kids cornflakes for breakfast. Pauls share this powerful domestic side. Together these two signs will make a beautiful, comfortable home.

Georges and Georges

A George paired with a George tends to be:

- Calm
- Uncommitted
- Stable
- Easy

Georges make for caring, stable, and dependable lovers. While they are not the most romantic sign in Beatleology, they are the least likely to show up naked at your work with your name painted on their buttocks. In other words, they aren't psycho lovers. Two Georges won't stalk, harass, or put the other's bunny in boiling water. A couple of Georges make for a calm relationship. They try to avoid conflict, especially in love and marriage. In fact, many Georges approach marriage as a way to simplify their lives; they no longer have to worry about Internet dating and other hassles of the single life. Ease is another component of a George-George relationship. Georges want things to be easy and laid back. They won't call at all hours of the night or get upset if you have a boys' night out with friends from work. In fact, they probably like having a night to themselves. Both will do everything in their power to avoid drama (another reason they should not date Pauls). They feel love and romance should be fun. However, due to this attitude, many Georges are not overly romantic. They aren't likely to write a love song or have "Lurlene" spelled out in skywriting on her birthday.

If two Georges are experiencing problems in their relationship it is unlikely either party will speak his or her mind for some time. Lack of communication is a common problem. Since this sign is highly passive, they are more likely to internalize any hurt feelings they may have. Georges will often overanalyze every aspect of the relationship in their head a million times before talking it out. If this couple learns to communicate and express their issues, they are capable of solving their problems calmly (unlike Johns and Pauls).

Georges can often be uncommitted in relationships. This isn't to say they are unfaithful—in truth they are highly monogamous—but they will have a hard time committing to a marriage or partnership. Many Georges aren't dying to get married. They may be too analytical about it or are often unsure of their desires. Georges have the tendency to ask "what if" all the time (What if I'd gone to a different college? What if we didn't get married?). Sometimes Georges just need to be pushed off the cliff since they approach life too safely.

Two Georges will enjoy a healthy sex life. This sign loves sex, especially with a willing participant. It is important, however, for both partners to be aware of their tendency to be too fetishistic. They may find themselves involved in swinging, S & M clubs, or foot fetishes. If this occurs, the couple may need to step back and have some good-old-fashioned-missionary-get-it-over-with-quick sex for a while.

Georges and Ringos

A George paired with a Ringo tends to be:

- Easygoing
- Communicative
- Highly sexual

George and Ringo couples are often highly successful in love. Like two Georges, a George-Ringo relationship is normally laid back and easygoing. Both partners have realistic expectations of the other and are comfortable giving space. These two signs are good at enjoying their time together without going overboard. They are also able to let go. If the George wants to visit her mother in Dallas for a week, the Ringo doesn't feel hurt. Both signs enjoy this trait in the other and will especially appreciate it if they've been with a Paul or John in the past.

Ringo brings more communication to the relationship than George. However, the George will often follow the Ringo's lead, creating a more communicative partnership. Ringos are good at expressing their feelings, which may, at first, put the George a little off balance. But soon, this sign will learn to reciprocate, allowing them to talk out any problems. The Ringo in the relationship must remember to ask the George if anything is wrong since this sign is more likely to internalize feelings and concerns. This couple is unlikely to write a great deal of love notes, but their day-to-day communication is unparalleled among Beatle Sign couples.

One nice aspect of a George-Ringo relationship is that they are highly sexual. Both signs love sex and are good at it. It is common for this couple to view sex as part of their recreation and as a reason they are together.

Ringos and Ringos

A Ringo paired with a Ringo tends to be:

- Unrestrained
- Loving
- Spontaneous
- Too casual
- Unfaithful

Two Ringos together in love make for a caring, doting, and sometimes unrestrained relationship. Ringos tend to be easy in love. They don't expect too much from their lovers and don't sweat the small stuff in a marriage. Unlike Johns and Pauls, they don't have unrealistic expectations of their partners. Ringos don't expect perfection, which keeps them from being disappointed. Two Ringos also make very loving couples. Neither partner will have a problem with affection. Luckily for the rest of us, they won't take this affection too far. Their love also has limits in private. Two Ringos are grateful for their partners, but they won't take that appreciation to an extreme. Ringos like things to be casual, especially in bed. Their sex lives will be fun and enjoyable but not overly dramatic. Ringos love sex, but they aren't hung up on it the way other signs can be.

A Ringo couple has the wonderful characteristic of being spontaneous. Unlike Pauls or Georges, this couple has no qualms about taking a long weekend and flying off to Cabo San Lucas for a little R & R. Often their spontaneity is in the form of a dinner out or romantic walk on the beach. But whatever it is, these two are able to forget their jobs and worries for a while. As one would expect, this only serves to strengthen their bond.

Unfortunately, for some of these relationships, things can get a little *too* casual. After the honeymoon period, they may begin to see their spouse as a roommate, not a lover. When dating, two Ringos have a tendency to call when it's convenient for them. Ringos should strive to keep their relationship alive.

Along with the Ringos' proclivity toward casualness comes the tendency to be unfaithful. This predisposition comes from a Ringo's laid-back attitude toward life and sex. If they aren't careful, they can be highly hedonistic and look for cheap thrills in the form of one-night stands or "friends with benefits." While it might be tempting for a Ringo to bang the coworker who keeps flirting with her, she needs to take the high road. Ringos don't have many negative traits, but this inclination runs strong in this Beatle Sign.

As previously discussed, Ringos have a strong need to create a tranquil home environment. Two Ringos will enjoy nesting in their home. They will enjoy those quiet moments like having coffee and reading the paper on Sunday morning.

Beatle Sex

The wonderful thing about sex, other than the act itself, is that an individual's sexuality is often unique, bizarre, and completely unrelated to their normal personality. That quiet, shy girl who works in accounts receivable may be a bondage freak on the weekend. Or the sales manager who loves his kids and being a daddy may make the Marquis de Sade look like Mother Teresa.

Each Beatle Sign has its unique qualities when it comes to sex. Each sign approaches sex differently. As with the personalities themselves, take into account ethnic, national, religious, and generational differences, but at their core these Beatle Signs share a lot of their sexuality.

Johns and Sex

Johns love sex. They love to get their rocks off and have a good time. Johns can also be lazy in bed. They are more than willing to let someone else do all of the hard work as long as they still get off. Johns have a kinky side, but usually it isn't too fetishistic.

For Johns, they want obtaining sex to be easy, too. Many are more than willing to have platonic sexual relationships to make their lives easier.

Pauls and Sex

Pauls are not overly sexual and tend to be the least sexually driven of all the Beatle Signs. They enjoy the adoration that sex brings (especially female Pauls). They also enjoy the cuddling afterward. Many Pauls use sex as a way to connect with their partner and keep him or her interested. By themselves, Pauls can often take or leave sex, which is not to say they don't enjoy it. They just aren't as sexually driven as Johns, Georges, and Ringos.

Georges and Sex

Surprisingly, Georges are highly sexual, often freakishly so. They love sex and seek it constantly. This is often in great contrast to their public personas. Many are surprised to find their George friends and coworkers lead a double life as a borderline sexual deviant. Georges need to abstain from overly fetishistic practices in their sex lives.

Georges, unlike Ringos and Johns, are generally very monogamous. They enjoy their hot sex lives in the context of a marriage or long-term partnership.

Ringos and Sex

Ringos are also highly sexual. They enjoy sex the way some enjoy watching football, riding dirt bikes, or playing video games; it's just something fun to do. Due to this, the Ringo sign is the most detached during sex. Many enjoy one-night stands, affairs, and even prostitutes since they don't always create an emotional bond during intercourse.

Ringos need to be careful not to use other signs just for sex, especially Pauls. At their best, Ringos participate in sex like hiking, a healthy and fun activity best enjoyed with your partner.

Famous Couples and Their Beatle Signs

Beatleology and Beatle Love have affected many famous couples throughout history. Many of those couples have had a deep and lasting impact on the world as we know it. Where would George Washington be without Martha? Or John Adams without Abigail? Or John Lennon without Yoko (well, two out of three ain't bad).

Take a look at these famous couples and how their Beatle Signs have affected history, politics, and art.

Adam (Ringo) and Eve (John)

Other than the Book of Genesis, little is known about Adam and Eve. We do know Adam was rather content just hanging out in the Garden of Eden with all the animals (a strong Ringo trait). Unfortunately, it was Eve (a classic John) who felt the need to upset the apple cart. Now, instead of living in Eden, we live in the suburbs (which is kind of like Eden only with a Starbucks on every corner).

George Washington (George) and Martha Washington (John)

George Washington's thoughtful, soft-spoken George nature is well known. He's an easy historical figure to identify. What is not well known is that Martha was definitely a John. On the positive side, she was a very dedicated spouse, spending the entire awful winter in Valley Forge with her husband. Like other Johns, she had some unfortunate lapses in morality. Martha owned over 100 slaves, including her own half-sister, Ann Dandridge.

John Adams (George with a John Rising) and Abigail Adams (Ringo)

John Adams was a serious, contemplative individual and not always well liked during his distinguished career (especially as an ambassador and even president). Abigail brought a grounded, supportive voice to his life. She was the sturdy weight that always dragged him back down to earth and consistently provided him with a much-needed sounding board.

Ike Turner (John) and Tina Turner (Paul)

In many ways, Ike and Tina Turner had a typical John-Paul relationship. Together they created some memorable music. Unfortunately, they also created an even more memorable abusive relationship. Ike, as the John, wanted to keep control over his more talented Paul wife, Tina. Luckily, Tina learned to assert herself and has never looked back.

Siegfried (Ringo) and Roy (Paul)

Siegfried and Roy met while working on a German ocean liner. Like a typical Ringo, Siegfried liked to perform magic in his spare time just for fun, but was soon allowed to have his own show on the ship. Roy had smuggled a cheetah onboard (a Paul's need to feel loved and adored often extends to animals). Together, they became some of the highest paid performers in the world. That is, until Roy's domineering Paul traits got him into trouble with a white tiger.

Bill Clinton (Paul) and Hillary Rodham Clinton (John)

With his charm, charisma, and way with the common man, Bill Clinton was obviously a Paul. His equally Machiavellian wife,

Hillary (an obvious John), has a harder time connecting with people. But like John Lennon and Paul McCartney, these two can do some wonderful things together.

Ozzy (Ringo) and Sharon Osbourne (Paul)

Anyone who caught an episode of *The Osbournes* knows Ozzy was the most normal, down to earth one of them all. So who made this typical Ringo become the reigning king of heavy metal? One word: Sharon. Sharon is a quintessential Paul. She is driven, pushy, and always demands her own way. Only she can make those tough rockers tremble in their boots.

Britney Spears (Ringo) and K-Fed (Ringo)

Too much has been written about these two rather untalented Ringos. Two Ringos can make for a great relationship, but it can also make for a lot of idiocy. Both of these Ringos lacked much responsibility (like putting a baby in a car seat). They are also seen as having little or no talent (other than the gift of publicity).

Kurt Cobain (John) and Courtney Love (John)

Kurt Cobain is obviously a John. He was a gifted songwriter and deeply troubled individual. Courtney Love was also a John, only without all of the talent. These two Johns occasionally brought out the worst in each other. Then like other relationships involving a John-John pairing, their relationship self-destructed.

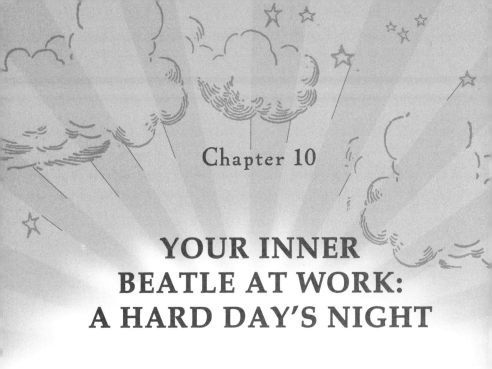

Chapter 10

YOUR INNER BEATLE AT WORK: A HARD DAY'S NIGHT

As with all aspects of life, Beatleology has a profound effect on our workplace. As anyone who has had a few jobs knows, work environments can vary greatly. This disparity is often due to the interplay of the Beatle Signs of our bosses and coworkers.

Your Beatle Sign's relationship to that of your boss can determine your success or failure in at work. Careers have been made and broken through Beatle Sign interaction.

Pauls tend to generate a lot of work output. Johns work best alone when hatching an idea and then benefit from the input of a group. Georges tend to be great workers, consistently producing well for the company, but are often overlooked for promotion in favor of their more outgoing coworkers. Ringos will sometimes be seat warmers at work, but seem always to do well in a corporate setting as they are non-threatening and well-liked.

Relationships between coworkers and bosses are determined by each individual's Inner Beatle and how they interact. A John supervising a George will be a positive combination; a George working for a Paul is a recipe for disaster. Bosses who are enlightened to the ways of Beatleology will compose teams of equal ratios of all Beatle Signs. This is a utopian state known as Equi-Beatle-librium.

In addition, a company has its own Beatle Sign. Disney is a classic Paul while GE is a George. Apple is a Paul, while Microsoft is obviously a George with a John rising. Enron was a Yoko to its employees and stockholders.

How Each Beatle Sign Fits into a Workplace

Just as each Beatle Sign plays a vital role in the Beatle-verse, the interaction of signs determines the success in the workplace.

Johns
At work Johns are usually:

- Creative
- Office clowns
- Hardworking
- Team builders

Johns are creative dreamers who contribute grand ideas. They are skilled at coming up with the big picture ideas but not with developing the fine details of a project. For example, in an architectural firm, a John would excel at the overall concept and theme of a building; but if he were put in charge of the details of the interior design, the building might end up with no bathrooms. Johns also have a tendency to think that all of their ideas are good ones. On the heels of the brilliant *White Album*, John and Yoko released their *Two Virgins* album, which was essentially screeching and sound effects recorded over the course of one night while the two were high as kites. John not only thought this was worthwhile material, but saw nothing wrong with stealing focus from the album that had been painstakingly crafted over the course of several months. Johns in the workplace need a strong Paul or George to filter their creative output.

Next among their positive traits is a John's ability to bring ideas and new ways of thinking to any workplace. They are creative and have the ability to think about problems in a unique fashion. A John is likely to suggest the company institute power naps and work-from-home policies. Another positive trait is a penchant for humor. Johns are very good at lightening the mood with a joke or funny e-mail. Like Georges, Johns are adept at finding the humor in any situation.

Johns should be careful not to tell sexist or racist jokes, especially in the workplace. Since Johns often lack a strong internal censor, they may be fired or face a sexual harassment lawsuit if they are not careful.

Johns can be highly diligent workers if they view their job as important. Many will put in long hours and take their work home without even being asked. However, if this sign views his work as demeaning or worthless, a John will often do only the minimum to avoid being fired. Bosses need to recognize this in their John employees and give them tasks of true value and importance. Last, Johns enjoy being "one of the blokes." They love having buddies and pals in the office, which helps with interpersonal relationships and networking.

Unfortunately, Johns bring a number of negative traits to the work environment as well. First, if a John doesn't care about his job, he's likely to do a great deal of ass-dragging from surfing the Internet all day to chatting with coworkers. A John who is trying to pursue a career as a painter can easily spend an entire workday doing absolutely nothing. Remember, Johns often lack a solid moral compass. Deep down, many don't care about their company, profits, or "being part of a team." Another troubling aspect is the tendency to believe everything they do is groundbreaking. Johns have to learn to bounce their ideas off coworkers and bosses. While a John might think it would boost morale to bring dogs to work, he needs to remember some people might be deathly allergic.

When working with a John, keep these facts in mind. First, it's important to let your John employee or coworkers express themselves. Even if you think their idea for a beer-vending machine in the break room is completely loony, you should remember to thank the John for her input and casually move on. A John can be a great contribution to any work environment, but it's essential to use him or her correctly.

Pauls

At work Pauls are usually:

- Creative
- Stubborn
- Team players
- Hardworking
- Popular
- Gossip mongers

While Pauls are also extremely creative and hardworking, they are stubborn and have a tendency to be control freaks. This sign tends to be tireless workers who believe in their company's infallibility. This trait sometimes annoys coworkers. A Paul working at McDonald's might have a picture of Ray Kroc hanging over his bed and happily sing the latest company jingle as he sweats over a grill while his disgruntled "team members" plot to lock him in the freezer. Heaven help them all if the Paul is promoted to assistant manager. Alpha Paul strove to be the popular front man of the group since he enjoyed the limelight. This trait should be harnessed in the workplace. A Paul would happily go on *60 Minutes* to defend her company's new diet soda that was responsible for the births of dozens of "tadpole babies," if it meant she could be on TV. Pauls in a subordinate position will tend to suck up to their boss, which can negatively affect their relationship with their fellow employees. All in all, Pauls are good to have in the workplace, but their gung-ho personality traits need to be kept in check. Pauls need some Johns around for the occasional reality check and dose of humility.

Pauls make great employees and supervisors. Their positives far outweigh their negative characteristics. Pauls are almost always dedicated to their job, no matter what it is. Even if they work at a sweatshop for nineteen cents an hour, they are devoted, reliable employees. This trait stays with them all the way up the management pyramid. Paul bosses are just as devoted to seeing the company succeed. Pauls will also put in countless overtime hours without being asked. They will work tirelessly to complete any task or project since a sense of accomplishment brings them great joy. Pauls also *believe* in their company. They actually believe the new Wal-Mart is good for his or her community.

Their negative aspects come mostly from interactions with coworkers. As we've seen, Pauls can be very pushy, especially at work. A Paul will think nothing of stepping on her coworker's toes to accomplish something. This can often alienate other Beatle Signs, especially Georges and Johns. A Paul's strong personality and need to dominate every meeting will cause tensions with many others in the workplace. Often, Georges may watch in silent frustration as a Paul steals all of her ideas and presents them to the company president. At the water cooler, a Paul will also dominate the discussion. For them it's all about me, me, me. A Paul won't care if your grandmother just went into the hospital; she watched the funniest episode of *The Bachelor* last night and just has to talk about it.

When working with a Paul, it is important to give him tasks and allow him to run with them. Rest assured, he will get the job done on time or early. Bosses who work with Pauls need to allow them a chance to voice their opinion but also make time for Johns, Georges, and Ringos. A Paul's coworkers must learn to let much of what she says just roll off their backs. It's not worth dwelling on what the Paul said since she probably forgot about it five seconds later, anyway.

Georges

At work Georges are usually:

- Consistent
- Stable
- Pragmatic
- Easy to get along with

Georges add a lot to the workplace. They are consistent, hard workers who tend not to cause trouble. They are often overlooked for recognition in favor of their flashier John, Paul, and Ringo coworkers. A CEO of the other three signs would be wise to keep a George as his right-hand man. The George would provide pragmatic grounding and non-butt-kissing advice when asked. Georges can see through the politics of the office and are generally above the fray. This is not always to their advantage since they do not form friendships and alliances easily. Georges need to be asked for their creative and managerial opinions since this opinion is usually well thought out and pragmatic. Had they been asked, in 1985 a George would have said "our company is successful beyond our wildest dreams in every nation on Earth by selling the same crappy formula of water and corn syrup we have for half a century. Let's not change anything." And New Coke would never have been born.

All successful businesses have many Georges as employees and managers. Georges make consistent and stable workers. They are always on time, if not early. While a Ringo might be great one day, and completely worthless the next, a George turns in quality work every time. They train easily and "get it." Georges are notorious for bringing a calm sense of sanity to their workplace. They don't get easily upset and are able to view things from a broad perspective. They avoid conflict and make an effort to be friendly with everyone on the staff (if that's possible). Last, Georges have a pragmatic approach to their jobs. In most cases, they want to avoid office politics and drama in order to get the job done.

On the negative side, if a George isn't careful, she can alienate herself from the rest of the employees. Many fellow workers may see her as arrogant or conceited. It is important for Georges to make some friends in the office. Georges can also hold a grudge more than any other sign in Beatleology. Unfortunately, Georges have the tendency to play both sides. Since they have the ability to move from one social circle to another, they make for excellent spies, which can occasionally foster resentment.

When working with a George it's important for coworkers and supervisors to give him or her a chance to be heard. Often, Georges have good ideas and suggestions that can be overshadowed by a Paul or John. Other Beatle Signs need to make an effort to include the George in the office social setting. Since they may alienate themselves, it's critical to ask them to participate in social functions.

Ringos

At work Ringos are usually:

> • Well liked
> • Grounded
> • Consistent
> • Popular

Generally, Ringos are good workers. They do their assigned task with skill and consistency. Ringos exceed when working with large concepts, but are not particularly talented as specialists. Skilled at networking, they are popular with coworkers and bosses alike. Ringos aren't perfectionists and don't believe in bringing work home with them. This balance of professional and personal life keeps them well grounded and avoids burnout. Though popular, a Ringo's contribution is sometimes overlooked, especially when it comes to accolades and promotion. Ringos are extremely loyal but also pragmatic. If they see a company floundering or their own career stalemated, a Ringo will not hesitate to change jobs; but they will not burn their bridges and always receive high praise from former employers. On the flip side, some Ringos will do only the minimum required. They see the higher profile Pauls and Johns in the company get all the credit and decide not to try. Ringos appreciate a steady job and are hesitant to set out on their own. The guy who quits his six-figure accounting job to become a street puppeteer is probably not a Ringo.

Ringos bring a great deal of positive traits to the workplace. Ringos are almost always popular and well liked. For any company, it's important to have employees who act almost as diplomats. Ringos have the ability to bring everyone in an office together. Many are above gossip and try to get along with everyone. Along with their magnanimity, Ringos make highly loyal employees. While they are not the hardest workers (see Pauls), Ringos are dedicated. They won't spend their days putting their resume on the Internet. However, bosses must realize their Ringo employee might be tempted away for more money and vacation time. Ringos are down-to-earth. They avoid drama and prefer life to be steady and even-tempered. This sign makes great office peacemakers and are commonly found working in human resources.

Unfortunately for corporations, Ringos are also inherently lazy. A Ringo will think nothing of coming in ten, fifteen, thirty minutes late to work. To them, being "on time" is a trivial matter. Many will do the minimum of work to avoid being fired. Ringo coworkers hate picking up his slack at work. Pauls will find themselves doing all of the filing or staying late to proofread the report a Ringo wrote in five minutes on a bar napkin. Another problem with Ringos stems from the fact that they are rarely talented in one particular area. While Georges make great C++ programmers, Ringos won't be nearly as proficient, preferring to organize the company softball game instead. Ringos make fantastic CEOs as they are good with the big picture, but lousy with the details.

When working with a Ringo, it's important to keep in mind the following ideas. First, if a Ringo is consistently late to work or takes a long lunch, it is a part of her nature. Just make sure she is still pulling her weight on a project. It's also important for bosses to keep a Ringo focused. Many Ringos would rather spend all of their time organizing the Super Bowl pool and sending invitations to baby showers. Fellow employees will need to get them on task. Pauls must learn that a Ringo takes his family and personal life very seriously. While a Paul will miss her daughter's piano recital in order to land a client, a Ringo will be out the door before the minute hand strikes five o'clock.

Alpha Beatles at Work

Ringo Starr, George Harrison, Paul McCartney and John Lennon, or "Alpha Beatles," had very different approaches to their jobs as composers and rock stars and played different roles in the working dynamic of the band.

Alpha Ringo

Ringo Starr was not a founding member of the Beatles; rather, he was invited to join just before the band's phenomenal success. First, Ringo was invited because he was an experienced and talented drummer. Second, he was nonthreatening, likable, and willing to take a subordinate role, which Pete Best was not. In the post-touring years, the Beatles took months in the studio to record an album due to excessive experimentation with sound, orchestration, and LSD. Ringo was known for laying down his drum track in one or two takes. He usually sat around while the others fooled around with recording effects and trying to get their guitar parts right.

Alpha George

George Harrison was significantly younger than John and Paul when he was allowed to join the fledgling Quarrymen. In those days,

John was the clear leader of the band and chose George because he could actually play the guitar with some proficiency. George's skill on the guitar made it possible for the band to survive the transition from skiffle to more mainstream rock-and-roll. As John and Paul became more musically sophisticated and their songwriting genius blossomed, George was pushed into the background. In the later years of the band, more of George's compositions made it onto the Beatles' albums. Alpha George's straightforward ballads and pop songs provided valuable balance to the increasingly psychedelic and experimental Lennon-McCartney compositions. Paul and George frequently locked horns over artistic and personal differences. George frequently felt his musical contributions to the group were overlooked.

Alpha Paul

Although Paul is still known as "the cute one," he was also "the pushy one." While John founded the group that would become the Beatles and acted as its clear leader, John became increasingly distracted with LSD, social protests, and Yoko Ono. The spotlight-hungry Paul moved in to fill the void as the group's leader, especially after the death of manager Brian Epstein. This was a double-edged sword. Immediately following the grueling recording of the brilliant and groundbreaking *Sgt. Pepper* album, Paul shanghaied the band into the asinine *Magical Mystery Tour* film. That movie is proof that everything only *seems* significant, deep, and clever when you're on drugs. Without Paul's initiative to instigate projects, the band might have broken up earlier than it did. On the other hand, had the Beatles taken a hiatus of a year or more, the band might not have burned out so quickly. Paul was a strong and motivating creative force behind the band, but he slowly cultivated resentment among the other members.

Alpha John

John Lennon founded the group and was arguably its artistic and social heart. In the beginning, young John saw the band as a way to gain social status and get girls. As the group gained popularity, it became Lennon's ticket out of a working-class existence he saw as tedious and demeaning. In the early years, John was desperate to make it and committed the band to a grueling performing schedule, sometimes doing three gigs a day. Later he was content to enjoy the fruits of his success and his desire to relax sometimes put him at odds with the restless Paul McCartney. After Brian Epstein's death and the formation of the Beatles' company, Apple Corps, John was key in resisting the temptation to compromise the band's counterculture image by cashing in on cheesy merchandise and business ventures. John was never content. Musically and socially, he pushed the Beatles to evolve from toe-tapping, bubblegum hits to musically groundbreaking concept albums. This evolution is the basis of the band's enduring legacy. In the end, however, John's self-destructive side and inseparability from Yoko contributed greatly to the wedge that eventually drove the Beatles apart.

TIPS FOR BEATLE EMPLOYEES

John

There's a fine line between brilliant and stupid. You will benefit from the input of your coworkers on projects. They can act as an important filter.

181

You have a predisposition to rash behavior. Wait at least twenty-four hours before you call or e-mail your boss to tell him what an SOB you think he is. Threats against the CEO's family are taken very seriously.

The Paul in your workplace will irritate you with her desire to control everything. However, she can be your biggest ally and creative collaborator. Try to keep your relationship with Pauls at work cordial even if you're not best friends.

You do not see why all work has to be done at the office. However, you will be expected to show up. Telling your boss that you missed work on Monday because you were in the bathtub all day coming up with a brilliant strategy to sell more widgets is not going to fly.

Honesty is a noble virtue, but only if you're on the witness stand. Everyone lies all the time to get along in life, especially at work. When casually asked "How's it going?" by the water cooler, don't answer: "I am adrift in a sea of bourgeois, soulless, capitalist pig culture surrounded by Philistines and I am debating how to kill myself."

Ally yourself with Ringos. You may be seen around the office as a creepy loner. Having a Ringo friend will draw you back into the mainstream of office culture where you can bag on the Pauls for being such kiss-ups.

Paul

You firmly believe that you should run everything and that you have a gift for always knowing what other people should do. Fight the urge to dominate everything at work. Take a moment to consider other people's input.

The Georges in the office may secretly hate your guts, and this can lead to passive-aggressive retaliation against you. Be secure in the knowledge that you are the greatest person who has ever lived and be charitable to office Georges.

If you've just fired a quarter of the employees and forced everyone else to take a pay cut, don't drive up the next day in a brand-new Ferrari you purchased with your bonus money.

It's handy to have a John around. Only she will have enough nerve to tell you some of your ideas aren't that great.

Some people in the company will see you as an overly enthusiastic boot-licker. Keep the fact that you have a company logo tattoo over your heart and that you baby-sit the boss's kids a secret.

Don't "charge the mound" at the company softball game.

George

Pauls will irritate you and try to steal your recognition. Avoid any actions of retaliation that will get you fired or put in jail.

You tend to do your job efficiently and not make waves. Because of this you do not have a very high profile in the company. Seek out Ringos as allies and don't be afraid to strive for recognition.

You are not going to get ahead by trying to be the brilliant loner in the company. Foster inner personal relationships.

You have a great many interests outside work and an inherent spiritual curiosity, but keep any really weird activities to yourself. For instance, if you and your spouse work part-time together as nude artist's models or if your church service involves handling poisonous snakes, keep it private.

Resist the temptation to only hang out with the other Georges at work.

Realize that there is a certain amount of politics and "getting along" in any workplace. Don't show up at your Vatican job with a pro-choice bumper sticker on your car.

You tend to be soft-spoken, friendly, and a good listener. Because of this, your coworkers and customers will try to get you to buy 500 boxes of their daughter's Girl Scout Cookies and join their latest pyramid scheme. Resist.

Ringo
You are sociable and well liked, but sometimes you are not taken seriously. Don't fall into the trap of being the office comedian.

Use your fun-loving personality to party with your supervisors. Sooner or later they will do or say something you can use as leverage at a later time. The threat of a shakedown is very powerful.

You don't define yourself as your job and you realize that there needs to be a balance in life. Your job needs to respect your time off. However, realize others are more fanatical about work and take care not to be seen as a seat warmer.

Ally yourself with Johns and Georges. The mix of their quiet creativity and your charisma will benefit everyone.

You believe that what you do outside work is your own business. This is fine, but realize that teaching elementary school and devoting your MySpace page to hardcore S & M can come back to haunt you.

Chapter 11

BEATLE FAMILIES: ALL TOGETHER NOW

Understanding your family dynamic and how it relates to your family members' Beatle Signs is critical for the happiness of any Beatleologist. Beatle Signs contribute to both functional and dysfunctional families. It's the combination of signs that can spell the success or doom of a family.

BEATLEOLOGY

This chapter will explore how the tendencies of each Inner Beatle affect the health, or pathology, of every family. It will also examine how your parents' Inner Beatles contributed to your relationship and shaped the person you are today. Lastly, Beatle families will discuss how Beatle signs affect sibling relationships.

Beatleology can help make all families more functional. The enlightened individual can use the principles of Beatleology to increase household tranquility and have a more meaningful and fulfilling relationship with family members. Taking into account your Beatle Sign and that of your family members is crucial to developing domestic peace. For instance, if you are a John and your spouse and children are all Ringos, without Beatleology, you would be likely to run the family car off a cliff while they sing "A Thousand Bottles of Beer on the Wall." But by recognizing your role as the thoughtful, somber one of the group, you can love them for who they are and avoid costly emergency room visits.

The optimal family would be comprised of equal numbers of each Beatle Sign, each sign making up for the weaknesses in the others. Such families are not immune to strife due to the diverse personalities involved, but as a healthy family unit it will have no equal. This balance is known as Equi-Beatle-librium and is very groovy.

All Inner Beatles play a crucial role in creating either healthy, functional families or big domestic disturbances. Harmony in the family comes from allowing the individual Beatle Signs to play their particular role in the family unit. The leopard can't change its spots and a Paul can't be a Ringo. Therefore, it's important to know how the pieces of your Beatle family fit together. Also, it's vital to know each sign's foibles to minimize strife. It doesn't matter what your

Beatle Sign is, you are capable of contributing both positively and negatively to your family. Remember, it's up to you how well your family gets along.

Johns and Family

In terms of Beatle family, Johns are the most dualistic of all the signs. Their approach to family can be either exceedingly hot or extraordinarily cold, depending on circumstances. That is why Johns can be very attentive family members or extremely distant and uncaring. For example, in John's first marriage to Cynthia, he was neglectful, distant, and resentful. Lennon was often an absent father and spouse, leaving Cynthia alone while he toured the world. John felt forced into marriage with Cynthia after learning she was pregnant. Just as Beatlemania was exploding, Lennon felt trapped and confined by his family. Since he secretly resented Cynthia and Julian, John felt no qualms about relentlessly cheating on her. Individuals with a John Beatle Sign can also exhibit these traits if they feel trapped or confined by their marriage.

 Positive Traits

Loving
Affectionate
Natural leader
Fun
Attentive (depending on family situation)

On the positive side, the other John, the one who feels stimulated by his or her marriage, can be the complete opposite of the "distant" John. This John is very loving and makes an attentive spouse and parent. Unlike his relationship with Julian, John completely embraced fatherhood when it came to his second child, Sean. The same can be said of his relationship with Yoko. Even before he and Yoko were married, the two spent nearly every minute of every day together. This is true of other John family members. Johns are often deeply involved with all of their family members, having a deep emotional bond with their spouse and children. When everyday Johns come to their family on their own terms, like having children when they are ready, they can be extremely tender and adoring.

In the domestic setting as well as at work, Johns have a tendency to be the family leader. Both male and female Johns like to be in charge. Johns prefer to set the family agenda whether it is vacation spots, weekend activities, or the dinner menu. When it comes to parenting, Johns like to think of the big picture but not take care of the details. For instance, a John mother is inclined to get her child involved in lessons, sports, and activities, but she will have a hard time arranging the carpool and remembering snacks.

 Negative Traits

Distant (depending on the family situation)
Mean
Philandering

Resentful

Codependent

Smothering

Unfortunately, John spouses and parents can be mean. John Lennon had a propensity toward cruelty. In his impressionable years, he was known for pranks and mean-spirited comments about the disabled and homosexuals. Other Johns have been known to make insensitive or belittling remarks (this is an especially dangerous trait for male Johns), which often negatively affects their spouses and children. When most kids bring home a picture they drew at school, a John will tell them what he or she really thinks, even if the child is only five years old.

John children are stubborn, mischievous, and conscious of social status. They will often dominate their siblings, especially if they are the oldest. Johns who are only children are in danger of developing a Jesus complex. A strong-handed Paul parent is often needed to rein in the willful John child.

Pauls and Family

Many Pauls embrace family life. To Pauls, having a loving, stable family plays an important role in their happiness and is a status symbol. This Beatle Sign makes for loving and protective spouses and parents who are involved in their children's lives. They are highly dedicated to their families. Pauls, like Johns, have an almost pathological need to be in charge. They can be pushy and prefer to dominate every family situation.

Positive Traits

Loving

Protective

Dedicated

Positive

Pauls enjoy the status and security that comes with a solid family. While they are loving and protective, they need a dedicated partner who reciprocates their feelings (it never hurts if they do exactly what the Paul says). Young Alpha Paul enjoyed his relationship with seventeen-year-old actress Jane Asher on several different levels. One, she was seventeen. Two, their relationship provided a certain amount of status for the budding rock star. Three, it exposed him to the cultural elite of London society. However, when Jane became too independent and assertive, Paul began to look elsewhere for the doting girlfriend who worshiped the ground he walked on. Luckily for Paul, in walked Linda Eastman who dedicated her life to loving him. Regular Pauls act much the same way. There is a certain amount of self-absorption in any Paul relationship. They often think, "What can my mate do for me?" But within that framework, they are loving and devoted. A Paul will treat his spouse like a goddess right up until the day he serves her with divorce papers and moves in with her sister.

As parents, they are highly supportive of their children, but also highly critical. Pauls are often seen coaching their son's T-ball team or helping their girls rehearse a pee-wee cheerleading routine. However, they are also likely to be the parents who scream profanity from the sideline when their son drops a fly ball.

 ## Negative Traits

Domineering
Pushy
Nitpicking
Stubborn

There's no doubt about it. Pauls like to have things their way. A John likes to be in charge, but is normally too lazy to worry about the details. Pauls also like to be in control, but have a need to dictate everything down to the smallest detail. They will make sure the car is gassed, snacks are packed, and music playlists are finalized, putting the more inspirational songs toward the end of the journey for dramatic effect. Occasionally, this pushiness rubs other family members the wrong way, especially if they are Georges and Johns. Neither of these signs likes to be told what to do.

Paul children are charming, but their charm lets them get away with murder. Often, a Paul is the pushiest child in the family and gets his or her way only because the squeaky wheel gets the grease. While Pauls often express a great deal of affection toward their parents, they have their own agenda. John children will be moody and openly oppose their parents. A Paul, however, comes off as amiable but does what he wants regardless of the rules. Paul McCartney was said to have had a 1,000-watt smile as a kid, but deep down he was a real terror and highly rambunctious.

Georges and Family

As one might expect, Georges make excellent spouses and parents, especially if their hearts and minds are really into being part of a family. George Harrison was a dedicated father and husband to both of his wives (who doesn't have a few divorces these days?). Harrison not only had a great relationship with his son, Dhani, but even recorded an album with him shortly before his death in 2001. Dhani often appeared on stage with his father showing that the two shared a close bond. Everyday Georges are similarly connected to their children if they choose to have them. Like Johns, if Georges are forced into having a family, they can be resentful. But generally, Georges have very positive relationships with their children. They aren't nags and rarely drive their children to therapy or cause them to develop eating disorders.

 Positive Traits

Stable
Understanding
Calm
Loyal

Georges make calm and stable spouses and parents. George households are not filled with screaming. You won't be awakened in the middle of the night by your neighbor Georges shouting and breaking beer bottles on each other's heads (those are usually Johns or Pauls). Most George couples are excellent at talking out problems but may hold resentments longer than they should. This is also true of their parenting. Georges don't scream and shake their children in Wal-Mart. They don't refer to them as a "stupid little bastard" during the conference with their kindergarten teacher (but they may be thinking it). Finally, Georges are highly stable individuals. This sign can be counted on to contribute to the family both spiritually and financially. Georges will work overtime to ensure young Susie can have braces.

 ## Negative Traits

Feeble

Disconnected

Distant

Noncommittal

Unfortunately, Georges can also be quite distant and disconnected from their spouses and children. If Georges are in a funk or are preoccupied by some project, they can be highly neglectful. It's not uncommon for Georges to miss birthdays and Valentine's Day if their mind is somewhere else. Spouses should remember to give friendly reminders about important dates or family events. In terms of parenting, Georges may be physically and emotionally distant from their children. Many Georges hate attending little league games or dance recitals, but risk alienating their children if they don't go. Sadly, many George parents have a hard time showing affection. They want to hug and squeeze their sons and daughters but don't know how.

"Dad, can we play with this wolverine we found in the backyard, make a bomb in the garage, and then run with scissors?"

"Sure. Just keep it out of the house."

Does that sound familiar? If you've allowed that kind of mischief and mayhem, you may be a George parent. George parents can be complete and utter pushovers and way too permissive. Georges don't have the strongest personalities and often let their kids get away with murder. This sign needs to remember to set and enforce boundaries for their children. Luckily, Georges rarely have crazy ADHD children because they were not that way themselves.

George children are often the quiet, dutiful kids in the class. They are respectful and try hard at school. For the most part, George kids toe the line. But parents need to be aware of their dark, hidden sides. Many George children are secretly growing marijuana in the basement or having sex with the football team. Parents of George children need to keep an eye out for their sneaky side.

Ringos and Family

Of all the Beatles, Ringo Starr was arguably the most family oriented. During the height of their popularity, while the rest of the Beatles were hobnobbing with celebrities, artists, and gurus, Ringo was content staying home with the wife and kids. While he enjoyed mind-altering experiences just as much as the next guy in the band, it was his family that really got him high. This is also true of Ringos in the everyday world. A great deal of a Ringo's happiness stems from his or her family. While many Ringos have a wide range of interests, they would much rather be hanging out with their spouse and kids than doing lines of blow off the bar with Robert Downey Jr. at the latest Hollywood nightclub.

Positive Traits

Loving
Dedicated
Kind
Involved

As both parent and spouse, Ringos are loving and dedicated. Known for giving and receiving affection, a Ringo father won't be afraid to hug his son or hold hands with his daughter. Ringo moms are all about love and affection. This trait is also true in the Ringo's marriage. They will often set a good example in front of the children, exhibiting hugs and kisses without any major groans from the kids.

It's almost an understatement, but Ringos are dedicated to their family. Most will do anything to ensure their safety and happiness. To them, family *is* their life, not just one element of it (which is often true for the other Beatle Signs). Even as their children reach adulthood, Ringos parents can be very supportive, from helping with rent to buying a keg for their graduation party.

Negative Traits

Permissive
Unfaithful
Apathetic

Like Georges, Ringos have the tendency to be very permissive parents. Ringo moms and dads are not concerned with things like "rules," or "boundaries," or "watching them in the swimming pool." That's just a drag. On the positive side, Ringo parents allow their children to take risks. They don't freak out over amusement park rides, running with rusty objects, or watching their kid climb high places. To them, that is how kids test life. On the downside, this Beatle Sign can permit too much. Ringo dads don't see why their thirteen-year-old son shouldn't be walking the streets of East L.A. alone at night. And a Ringo mom can't find a reason her thirteen-year-old daughter shouldn't date that nice twenty-one-year-old she met in rehab. Children will quickly learn to ask their Ringo parent if they can light something on fire.

This permissive streak can interfere with the spousal relationship as well. A Ringo doesn't want to seem as if she's keeping tabs on her husband, but she needs to start asking questions when he comes home late from work smelling like a French cat house. Often, Ringo spouses need to learn to ask questions and show concern if there are issues within the marriage.

Ringo children are often high-energy, good kids. They rarely get into any major mischief at home or at school. Ringo kids tend to be popular and get along well with their siblings.

How to Deal with Your Parents' Beatle Sign

For both young and adult children, dealing with your parents is a fact of life. You're stuck with your parents until death, or at least until you can get them committed to a home. Therefore, learning how to deal with their Inner Beatle is essential. The different combinations of your parents' Beatles Signs dramatically influence your relationship. No two groupings are the same.

John and John Parents

Having two Johns as parents can either be a blessing or major disaster. If they made the conscious decision to have kids, you're in luck. When Johns want children, they are creative, dedicated parents. They regularly read to their kids, take them to zoos and aquariums, or work on art projects together. However, if your John mom and dad were forced into parenthood, you may be out of luck. Johns can be notoriously self-absorbed. They may even resent your existence. This will manifest itself as acting distant and indignant over the duties of parenthood. If your John-John parents are codependent, they may neglect you altogether. Johns in this situation are selfish and want to spend all of their time with their partner.

Under the right circumstances, Johns raise free-thinking and creative children. Their kids are often brilliant, but slightly troubled. Children brought up by two Johns tend to go into nontraditional lines of work or community service.

John and Paul Parents

It can be difficult having John and Paul parents. Both can be quite intense and demanding. Their relationship to each other often takes center stage, leaving the kids out of the picture. This is not to say that the children of these two Beatle Signs will not be well loved. Both Johns and Pauls have a strong need to give and receive love, which they will impart to their children. This can manifest both positively and negatively. If the couple is working together, the kids will benefit greatly. If they are at each other's throats, or divorced, the kids can get caught in a game of one-upping the other. "If your mother loved you as much as I do, she would take you to Disneyland, too," or "Your father would come to your recital, but I guess he doesn't love you." This behavior often strains the children or insures they will be receiving therapy well into their forties.

Johns and Pauls have radically different parenting styles. The Paul parent will generally be more demanding and set high expectations for children. Pauls are better at setting boundaries and expect their children to be kind, respectful little people. Johns, on the other hand, are by far much more permissive. This can lead to many rifts over parenting styles.

Children of a John-Paul couple should be aware that if the marriage starts to go south, they can be in for a great deal of trouble. A John-Paul marriage can be fantastic or a fantastic train wreck. Sadly, if their relationship is disintegrating, it's the children who will be neglected. They will also be used as a weapon against the other adult. Older and adult children who find themselves in this situation need to remember to stay neutral and supportive. Stuart Sutcliffe and Astrid Kirchherr were a John and Paul, respectively, and a good example of how that pairing can sometimes be a positive one.

John and George Parents

John and George parents can be a very positive pairing. These two Beatle Signs have very different strengths and weaknesses that can offset each other. The John parent is in a unique position as both the fun parent and the disciplinarian due to the George parent's steady but hands-off parenting style. The John parent will generally be the more dominating parent, and this can lead to interesting highs and lows in child rearing. A John is likely to convert the basement into a lavish Japanese dojo complete with miniature ninja weapons after his child's first karate lesson. Then a week later, he'll convert it to a pool after the kid quits karate and takes up swimming. The

George parent's steadier approach is needed to balance out the highs and lows of the John. The George parent needs to make a conscious effort not to be completely dominated by the John.

John and Ringo Parents

Perhaps the best pairing for raising offspring, a John and Ringo will have an excellent chance at a happy home and happy children. A Ringo's positive, pragmatic, family-oriented personality will complement a John's highs and be able to pick up the slack for his or her lows. A Ringo will be able to "put up with" a John and give her the space she sometimes needs. Conversely, the John has the drive to follow through with tasks and get things accomplished, when she feels like it, that the Ringo may lack. A John parent might get up in the middle of the night and plan an entire family road trip from Atlanta to Mount Rushmore, along with accommodations, points of interest, projected gas mileage, and a schedule of bathroom breaks and then lose interest in the trip. The Ringo parent would then pick up the slack and have the steadiness to follow through with the project and handle the more mundane tasks of packing the bags and remembering little Billy's asthma inhaler. A Ringo-John couple will be able to give their kids the space they need to develop, although they could give too much space and find little Billy running an illegal underground craps game in the garage without their knowledge.

Paul and Paul Parents

When you see a twelve-year-old gymnast in the Olympics who has been training fourteen hours a day with a private Romanian coach for the past ten years, do you ever wonder about her parents? Your answer is two Pauls. Pauls are intense and goal oriented; they like things their own way. Two Paul parents will tend to have immaculate homes and intelligent, talented children; they will also be closely involved in their lives and activities. They run the risk of being too intense and cause rebellion and burnout, especially if their kids are Johns or Georges. A John child of two Pauls will see his parents as uptight and pushy and tend to withdraw into his own introverted activities such as Dungeons & Dragons, ships in a bottle, or online credit card fraud. George children will try to please their parents as long as they can but then burn out in a dramatic fashion. The valedictorian, class president, and captain of the cheerleading squad who freaks out senior year and runs away to Yemen to become the thirty-seventh wife of an eighty-five-year-old is probably a George with Paul parents. Jane Asher, who Paul almost married, was a Paul herself. Pauls love themselves so this relationship was very passionate until the overabundance of Paulness caused their split.

Paul and George Parents

This combination can spell trouble. In the later years of the band, Paul and George had an increasingly antagonistic relationship, with Paul taking over the leadership of the group from the drugged-out John. George resented this and had difficulty asserting his independence. Similarly, a husband and wife Paul and George will start their relationship in a positive way, but as time wears on the George will be less likely to put up with the Paul's dominance. George or Paul children of this pairing will tend to side with the parent of the same Beatle Sign, which can increase the conflict. Ringo children will fare the best and the addition of a Ringo to the family introduces much-needed balance. Heather Mills, with whom Paul had a short, disastrous, and expensive marriage, was a George.

Paul and Ringo Parents

This pairing will usually turn out well. The fun-loving, laid-back Ringo will balance out the more intense Paul and still be able to put up with the Paul as time goes by. The Paul will fall into the role of leader, but the Ringo will have enough perspective to contribute to the relationship and flourish without being dominated. As parents, the Paul will be the disciplinarian and the Ringo the favorite. All Beatle Sign children will do relatively well with Ringo-Paul parents as there is enough variety in their personalities to connect on some level with just about anyone. A John child will be nurtured by this combination particularly well and can often achieve great things and the modicum of peace that is difficult for restless Johns. Alpha Ringo's second wife, Barbara Bach, is a Paul, and Paul McCartney's first wife, Linda, was herself a Ringo.

George and George Parents

Georges paired with Georges will be stable and productive but can lack passion and spontaneity. Georges have a great capacity for love, but two Georges can be too shy and uncommunicative to express their feelings for each other. Georges make good parents. They are caring and consistent and take an interest in their children's lives without being overbearing, but sometimes they have trouble showing affection. Johns need constant affirmation and John children can feel disconnected if their parents are both Georges. A family of all Georges will get along well but can lack intimacy. Paul children will naturally try to dominate their George parents while a Ringo adds just the right element for a balanced family life. Pattie Boyd and Olivia Arias, Alpha George's first and second wives, are both Georges.

George and Ringo Parents

Have you ever met a couple where one partner is fun-loving, verbose, and loves to socialize and the other partner is quiet and shy, but ultimately runs the show? If so, you're probably dealing with a George and Ringo. A Ringo's warm, outgoing nature generally pairs well with the more thoughtful and mentally organized George. Georges are very spiritual, and if they are strictly religious this can cause conflict with the more "what you see is what you get" Ringo. Children with all four Beatle Signs have a good chance at fulfillment. Johns and Pauls will have a particular opportunity for self-expression and nurturing with George-Ringo parents. Alpha Ringo's first wife, Maureen, was a George, and the two had a very successful family life, until their divorce in 1975.

Ringo and Ringo Parents

If you've ever seen a seventy-year-old couple on his and hers motorcycles pulling into a bingo parlor, you've probably witnessed two Ringos. Generally speaking, two Ringos have the best chances of any Beatle Sign paired with itself. A Ringo-Ringo couple will be the life of the party as well as fun, loving, and engaged parents. However, Ringo couples can also exaggerate their negative traits. Ringos love a good time and are happy with what they have in life, but this sometimes leads to apathy when it comes to providing financially for the family. Ringos are dearly loved by their children, but sometimes they fail to give the guidance and discipline necessary. Every Fourth of July (or other holiday involving fireworks such as Chinese New Year, Boxing Day, or Yom Kippur), there is a story of an unsupervised eleven-year-old who blows off his thumb while his parents are passed out drunk at the trailer park party.

These parents are usually Ringos. On the other hand, the million-aire snowboard champion whose parents let her drop out of school and move to Colorado when she was sixteen probably has Ringo-Ringo parents, too.

Sibling Beatlery: Dealing with Beatle Brothers and Sisters

Johns

Johns are moody and rebellious but crave attention. They are often the black sheep of the family causing them to be the center of attention. Other siblings, especially Pauls, will naturally resent this. However, it will take some of the pressure and scrutiny off the other signs. Ringos in particular may seize upon this to get away with murder and still look like the model child. Pauls will sometimes react to John siblings by becoming the "anti-John," the insufferably perfect valedictorian, wrestling team captain, and church youth group leader.

Pauls

Pauls have just as much of a dark side as Johns, but they express it in different ways. Pauls love to get what they want and use charm and deception as opposed to outright rebellion. Eddie Haskell from *Leave It to Beaver* was a Paul. Pauls who are the oldest child will tend to lord it over their younger siblings. They will frequently set an impossible example by being the "Mr. Perfect" that their brothers and sisters can never live up to. Youngest child Pauls will feel everything they do is Masonic and that they all are the centers of the universe. These children consider themselves infallible and don't mind making everyone else aware of this. Many a religious leader who makes a vitriolic condemnation of sinners but is eventually discovered to have a personal life that would make the Marquis de Sade blush is frequently a youngest child Paul.

Georges

George children can be introverted and are sometimes neglected in a family situation especially if surrounded by children of more high-maintenance Beatle Signs. Georges can be the solitary nerdy child who is at his computer eight hours a day until becoming a billionaire at seventeen by creating a new website. While quiet and shy, Georges do not like to be dominated. This can lead to conflict, especially with Paul siblings. Heaven help the George middle child whose older sibling is a Paul and younger sibling a John. Sandwiched between two high-profile, dominant Beatle Signs the George is liable to be a real Nowhere Man, neglected, forgotten and in danger of being accidentally abandoned at an amusement park.

Ringos

Everyone loves a Ringo. While not the sharpest kid on the playground, Ringos enjoy good relations with siblings. Ringos are comfortable with who they are and are willing to except the manic-depressive Johns, Napoleonic Pauls, and reclusive Georges for who they are and therefore are accepted in the same spirit. Families in which the oldest child is a Ringo are particularly fortunate. First of all, the parents will enjoy the young Ringo enough to keep having children (this doesn't always happen with Johns). Second, this eldest Ringo will set a loving, laid-back example for his or her younger siblings. Youngest child Ringos will tend to be slackers but will be well loved and will always have a sibling or two around to borrow money from and crash on their couch.

Children

While a child can be born with any Inner Beatle, one's Beatle Sign is often influenced by those of the parents. Each Beatle Sign tends to give birth to certain signs. While these tendencies are by no means set in stone, they should be considered before making the decision to have children.

Johns

Johns tend to have John or George children. This rather intense Beatle Sign will either give birth to smaller versions of themselves or kids who are a slightly more toned-down George. It is rare for Johns to have Paul children.

Pauls

Pauls, of course, tend to sire other Pauls. Extroverted, popular, and strong people tend to give birth to other extroverted, popular, and strong people. Surprisingly, they will occasionally have John kids. Since both Johns and Pauls are strong signs, it isn't uncommon for a Paul to have a strong, but more intense and troubled, John child.

Georges

Like Johns, Georges tend to produce kids who are either Georges or Johns, with the former being a more likely possibility. It's rare for a George to have a Paul child, unless the other parent is a Paul.

Ringos

Ringos will often have children of any sign. The majority of the time, their child's Beatle Sign will be determined by that of the other parent (assuming they are not a Ringo themselves).

Where do all the Ringos come from? You may have noticed most signs do not tend to give birth to Ringos. So, how do we get them? Ringos come from an odd marriage or coupling. For instance, George W. Bush and Laura Bush gave birth to a Ringo-like Jenna. As another example, only an odd couple like John F. Kennedy and Jackie could have a Ringo child like John-John.

Chapter 12

HISTORICAL BEATLES: LADY MADONNA

Everyone knows the outcome of world events are determined by the people involved.

World War II may not have been a horrific catastrophe if it hadn't been for personalities like Hitler, Goering, and others. Similarly, the American Revolution may not have been successful if not for Thomas Jefferson, John Adams, George Washington, and James Madison. It is now clear that the participants' Beatle Signs had a great impact on those historical events.

This also holds true for other cultural areas such as fine art, music, theater, and literature. Picasso might not have had such an impact on the art world if he had not been an Inner John. If Picasso had been a Ringo, he might have been content painting sea shells down in Key West.

As you can plainly see, the Inner Beatle of celebrities and historical figures has shaped our world into what it is today. This chapter will explore how Beatle Signs have fashioned world events and the arts.

Historical Events

The Fall of Rome

No one individual can be blamed for the fall of ancient Rome. But as a collective group, the citizens and leaders of the most powerful city-state share the blame. Basically, it comes down to this: Rome, if it had a collective Inner Beatle, would be a Ringo. Remember, if left unchecked by another Beatle Sign, Ringos can become highly hedonistic and neglect the more important aspects of life. Romans became too caught up in consuming copious amounts of wine, watching gladiator spectacles (a.k.a. reality TV), and neglecting their empire. Had Rome been a George or a Paul, it might have ended up more like a London, Prague, or Des Moines.

World War II

There were many strong and important personalities involved in World War II. It was a complex series of events that shaped the world. The central figure, Adolf Hitler, was a John to an extreme degree. He possessed all of the negative traits, including insanity, lack of morals, a raging ego, and a desire to set the world on fire. This led to the armed buildup of Germany; his expansionist views and sense of entitlement; the invasion of Poland, Russia, and other countries; and the concentration camps. Hitler's reign ended in the death of millions of innocent people, the destruction of Germany, and his suicide. Had Hitler been a Paul or Ringo, he might have been content staying in Austria and churning out bad paintings of Vienna.

Cuban Missile Crisis

During the Cuban Missile Crisis, John F. Kennedy, who was a classic Paul, squared off with Nikita Khrushchev, a John. The strong signs of John and Paul are very reactive and could have led to disaster. Both signs demand to have their way and rarely back down in a fight. Being a Paul, Kennedy took more of a populous approach to solving the problem than did Khrushchev. From their conflict, some of the first Cold War compromises between the two nations were created. Johns and Pauls will butt heads, but together they can do incredible things.

The Kennedy Assassination

Anyone who was alive during the Kennedy assassination remembers exactly what they were doing when they heard the news. As with all world events, the Beatle Sign of both John F. Kennedy and Lee

Harvey Oswald play a major role in how the moment transpired. We now know that Lee Harvey Oswald was obviously a John. He was a deeply troubled man and had an unrealistic sense of self-importance. And like other Johns, he couldn't stand one particular Paul. In this case, that Paul was John F. Kennedy.

Vietnam War

The Vietnam War is a classic example of ego, hubris, and judgment gone horribly awry. Much of the death and destruction could have been prevented had the personalities involved let go of their sense of "honor" and done the right thing. Lyndon Johnson's Inner Beatle was a Paul. As a result, he liked to be in charge and have his way. He also rarely admitted mistakes, like escalating an unwinnable war. Had Johnson been a George or Ringo, he would have taken more time worrying about the ramifications of the war and less about his legacy. When the war was handed off to Richard Nixon (a John), his ego and lack of moral compass only compounded the situation.

Historical Figures

Christopher Columbus

If many famous explorers appear to be Pauls, it's no coincidence. It takes a very specific personality type to lead a ship into uncharted waters, claim land already occupied by other people as their own, take some as slaves, and try to convert the others to Christianity. Columbus did all of those things, without ever feeling remorse for the capture and eventual death of his slaves.

Napoleon

Despite conquering half of Europe and naming himself Emperor of France, Napoleon had a major Napoleon Complex (you'd think his parents would have thought of that before naming him Napoleon). Ascribed to his short stature, Napoleon suffered from inferiority complexes and a lack of self-esteem—this clearly makes Napoleon's Beatle Sign a John.

Samuel Adams

The brewer and patriot Samuel Adams was classic American Paul. Sam Adams was much more outspoken than his cousin John (a George) and much less cerebral. He helped to organize the Boston Tea Party out of patriotism and to keep his smuggling business afloat. At the First and Second Continental Congress, he advocated independence from the British Crown. This outspoken man of action was most definitely a Paul.

Martin Luther King Jr.

Another famous Paul of the twentieth century was Martin Luther King Jr. Like all Pauls, he believed deeply in his particular cause. He was also a profoundly religious and spiritual man, which are often attributes of Pauls. Additionally, MLK, like all Pauls, was a highly popular person. Dr. King used his charisma and allure to bring people together.

Mao Zedong

Like Paul McCartney, Mao had humble working-class origins and rose to international fame. He changed the world with his ideas and, like other Pauls, wanted everyone to believe exactly as he did. As stated before, Pauls are one of the strongest signs in all of Beatleology. Mao was so strong, he felt others must believe in his ideals completely or be "re-educated." Even after his death, Mao's personality still permeates Chinese culture.

Magellan

While many of Magellan's beliefs and behaviors could be seen as John-esque, this famous explorer was clearly a Paul. As Magellan discovered new lands and cultures, his sense of self-importance increased exponentially. He ruled his fleet with an iron fist and demanded his way. Finally, believing he could not be defeated, he charged into battle where he was killed.

Cicero

Cicero was a gifted statesman, orator, and writer. In a time of bloody villains like Mark Antony and murderers like Brutus, Cicero was a patient, philosophical man. These facts put him squarely in the George category. Cicero was an idealistic thinker who championed a return to the republic in the face of Caesar's dictatorship. He was also very sharp with his pen, writing numerous philosophical and rhetorical books.

Harry Truman

It's hard to imagine many modern-day presidents being soft-spoken and thoughtful like Harry S Truman. Truman was indeed a George. He had a certain quiet charm, but was able to assert himself after taking office in 1945. Intellectually, Truman was a man ahead of his time, advocating national health insurance and civil rights.

Like many Georges, he had high ideals but was often met with a great deal of resistance.

Abraham Lincoln

Abraham Lincoln was a thoughtful, intellectual, moral, and occasionally depressed man. Lincoln is a classic George, much in the same way as John Adams. For Lincoln, the Civil War went beyond a political struggle; it was a human struggle. While not generally believed to be religious, his George-like spirituality manifested itself as a strong sense of morality.

Gandhi

The fact that he was an Indian, coupled with his peaceful protests, makes Mahatma Gandhi a George. As with other Georges, Gandhi was obviously highly spiritual and religious. He also played a key role in nonviolent protests in India and South Africa, a sense of dedication only attributed to Georges and Johns.

The Buddha (Siddhartha Gautama)

Georges are known for their deeply philosophical sides. Many take religion and spirituality very seriously, but they are not mindless followers. This is an especially good trait for someone who went on to found his own religion. Siddhartha, known as the Buddha, was most definitely a George. Despite being born into royalty, Siddhartha was not spiritually fulfilled and left his easy life to find the universal truth that life is suffering. Siddhartha's words and teachings helped found one of the world's major religions (and gave Richard Gere something to do).

George Washington

As his name states, George Washington was a George. He was soft-spoken, thoughtful, and had a strong sense of ethics. While he wasn't the loudest voice in the Revolution, he was often the most powerful. This George could inspire men to follow him, but didn't hesitate to pitch in when it was required.

Malcolm X

Malcolm X spent his formative years as a petty criminal (as do many Johns); it wasn't until prison that he accepted Allah. Like other Johns, when he found religion, Malcolm didn't become just a casual, everyday Muslim. No, he jumped in with both feet and joined the Nation of Islam (which is also full of Johns). While Malcolm fought for civil rights, he often referred to whites as "devils." Be that as it may, this duality is often characteristic of Johns; on one hand, they can be significant, thoughtful people, and on the other, they can be a little over the top.

Pol Pot

As we've seen, Johns are very good at instigating major economic and political change. Unfortunately, like Pol Pot and the Khmer Rouge, they are also adept at genocide and mass murder. Johns like Pol Pot, who find themselves in a position of absolute power, as tempting as it may be, should think twice before executing an estimated 3 million people.

Nero

Since the historical record isn't entirely clear, Nero is assumed to be a Paul. As the last Roman emperor, it is said Nero was obsessed with his popularity. He even passed laws forbidding people to talk badly of him. During much of his rule, he spent a great deal of time visiting brothels and taverns (possibly giving him a John minor sign). Once Nero gained the throne, he was often ruthless in his methods for consolidating power. Like any good Paul, to Nero, having absolute power was a rush. Finally, the people rebelled causing Nero to (reportedly) commit suicide.

Che Guevara

Che Guevara is yet another dualistic John. Not only was he a leftist revolutionary dedicated to empowering the poor, he was also a doctor who traveled throughout Latin American to provide medical care to the impoverished. What many don't realize is he also had a darker side. During the Cuban Revolution, Guevara was a harsh military commander and often executed deserters. After the revolution, he was instrumental in bringing nuclear missiles into the country, prompting the Cuban Missile Crisis. The fact that one man could be so good and yet so cruel and shortsighted proves Che had to have been a John.

Joseph McCarthy

Like many Johns, Joseph McCarthy lacked a strong moral compass and often abused alcohol. Anyone with a strong sense of right and wrong (practically everyone shy of Hitler and Stalin) would have seen his hearings as self-serving. But many Johns don't see a problem with anything that benefits their agenda.

Current Events (the Past Twenty Years)

O. J. Simpson Trial

In the world of jurisprudence, no case is more iconic than the first O. J. Simpson trial. The different Beatle Signs were pitted against each other in a courtroom drama. O. J. Simpson was an obvious Paul who thought he could play by his own rules and not suffer the consequences. He was aided by Johnnie Cochran, a Ringo, known for his flashy style and charisma. Marsha Clark and Christopher Darden were Johns, searching for social justice and the truth. This was a classic John versus Paul clash of wills. Judge Ito was a George who was unable to control the Paul in the courtroom. Obviously, the participants' Beatle Signs played a crucial role in determining the outcome of the case.

Iraq War

The decision making behind the Iraq War came down to a poor mix of Beatle Signs. Had the architects of the conflict had different Inner Beatles, the United States may not have gone to war and then managed it so poorly. The problem stemmed from George W. Bush's Ringo sign. A negative trait of Ringos is that they can be easily led by the more serious and dominating signs in Beatleology. Dick Cheney, a quintessential John with his lack of a moral compass and empathy, lead the president into an ill-conceived war. He was aided by two Pauls (Donald Rumsfeld and Paul Wolfowitz) who often have a hard time apologizing or admitting mistakes.

2000 U.S. Presidential Election

The hotly contested presidential election of 2000 pitted a Ringo (George W. Bush) against a George (Al Gore). While some believe the Supreme Court decided the outcome, we know their Beatle Signs had decided the outcome long before the first votes were counted. As with most Georges, Al Gore approached the problem of the recount intellectually; he knew there procedures and laws to be followed and expected they would turn out in his favor. George W. Bush, on the other hand, approached the recount as a classic Ringo. He knew it was an emotional issue to be won using the heart, not the mind. The Republicans launched into a public relations attack that made Al Gore into a thief, not someone who wanted to see democracy run its course.

Abu Ghraib Prison Scandal

They say a photo is worth a thousand words. Witness the Abu Ghraib prison scandal story, which first broke in 2004. Specialist Lynndie England exhibited traits common to a Ringo. She was just a dumb kid having a good time and following the lead of her superiors like Specialist Charles Graner. Graner, a John, lacked a solid sense of morality and had tortured prisoners in both Iraq and the United States (allegedly); charges were dropped when his accuser disappeared). England followed the lead of the more dominant Graner and got caught up in his cruel treatment of the prisoners. Had England been a George, Paul, or John, she may have had a greater sense of self and refused to participate in the abuse.

Barack Obama and Hillary Clinton Primary Campaign

This battle for the democratic nomination was a classic battle of a John versus a Paul. While the Paul (Obama) was generally better liked, the John (Clinton) had a certain dominance and wouldn't let go. If only these two could have found a way to work together, they might have had that classic Lennon-McCartney spark.

George W. Bush

There's no doubt about it; George W. Bush is a Ringo. Throughout his career, he's exhibited many Ringo traits. First, until recently, Bush has always been extremely well liked. Nobody knows why, but there's just something about the guy that everybody loves (maybe it's the nicknames). Unfortunately, Ringos are also easily led by Pauls and Ringos (see Iraq War). Ringos, like President Bush, aren't overly analytical and don't look at things like facts, data, or military intelligence. They like to go with their gut.

Nelson Mandela

Nelson Mandela just goes to show what a John can accomplish when he uses his power and convictions for good. After one day in prison, much less twenty-seven years, most of us would give up on our cause—but not Mandela. He spent his life ensuring black South Africans had equal rights and a voice in their democracy.

Richard Nixon

Nixon was most definitely a John. He was highly intelligent, cunning, and cutthroat, and he lacked any sense of morality. Like many Johns, if Nixon had put his gifts of acumen to good use, he could have been a great president. Instead, Tricky Dick was more concerned with keeping and consolidating power.

Jimmy Swaggart

Jimmy Lee Swaggart exemplifies what it is to be a John. While no one can doubt his passion about Christ and his teachings, we can't be so sure about his sense of morality and decency. Not only did he expose fellow televangelists and their indiscretions (possibly to consolidate his own power), he was caught with a hooker in a cheap motel. Interestingly, while he was a regular client she claimed they never had regular intercourse. Be that as it may, we don't think they were just praying together.

Rupert Murdoch

Many see this media mogul John as a poster child for why we need independent, unconsolidated media outlets. Murdoch, like other Johns, has conservative views that many find misguided. When it comes to buying corporations and consolidating his power, he has an insatiable appetite.

Ted Bundy

In many ways Ted Bundy was similar to Richard Nixon. Both of these Johns had gifted minds but lacked a moral compass. Unfortunately, Ted Bundy's immorality manifested itself as serial killings. All Johns should be aware of the little voice inside their heads telling them to do things that are highly illegal.

Richard Branson

While most billionaires are content lighting cigars with $100 bills and eating poor African orphans for breakfast, Branson has decided to become an adventurer and pioneer. Branson (no relation to the city in Missouri) participates in activities and ventures, which have made him a household name. While most Pauls can't be famous, all Pauls like to be known and have a reputation for wonderful things. Along with his Paul-esque charm, Branson is also a ruthless businessman. His Virgin label now controls more than 360 companies worldwide. Only a Paul could do that.

Monica Lewinsky

Like many Pauls, Monica just wanted to be loved. She really felt that as a twenty-one-year-old intern, she could have a relationship with the most powerful man in the world . . . and that he really felt "all the time we spend together is special." Of course, Monica was drawn to Clinton's power and charisma.

Steve Jobs

The creator of the Macintosh, iMac, iPod, iPhone, and iYuppie could only be a Paul. Pauls, like Jobs, are trendsetters. They want the world to think as they do. They are nonconformist in a conformist sort of way. Many CEOs are Pauls, and Jobs is no exception. They must have a certain self-confidence and sense of entitlement that allows them to earn $100 million a year without feeling guilty.

Osama bin Laden

The leader and founder of Al-Qaeda just has to be a Paul. He's very religious (some may say a little too religious), he wants to be popular, and he's definitely one of those "my way or the highway" type of guys. While his actions and beliefs are repulsive, it is undeniable that he has a certain charm and charisma (that attracts other nuts). This is true of many Pauls, but they tend to use their appeal to get friends and dates.

Kim Jong Il

Kim Jong Il may not seem like it, but he's a Paul. First of all, he likes to be in charge and doesn't care if he rules with an iron fist. Second, he loves trendy American things like bad action movies, iPods, and pop music.

John Ashcroft

While it hasn't been officially confirmed, John Ashcroft can only be a Paul. It takes a Paul to believe he is universally loved and doing the Lord's work when he covers up naked statues of Lady Justice. It also takes a Paul to get up in front of the press and sing bad songs: "*Let the eagle soar, like he's never soared before. . . .*"

Barack Obama

Obama's cheery optimism and popularity make him a Paul. Like many Pauls, people are just drawn to his charm and charisma for reasons they don't even know. He is always the star attraction whenever he enters a room.

Ross Perot

Ross Perot and his Ringo Inner Beatle shook up the 1992 presidential campaign. His down-to-earth charm and colloquial way of speaking won over millions of fans and voters. He was short, a little strange, and not particularly good looking. But, like other Ringos, he captured America's attention and almost the White House.

Tony Blair

Tony Blair is often thought of in the same vein as Bill Clinton, but while these two world leaders have many similarities, they possess very different Beatle Signs. Tony Blair, contrary to popular opinion, is a Ringo. The Right Honorable Mr. Blair has a great deal of charisma. Like many Ringos, he has an informal manner and seems highly approachable though he was one of the most powerful men in the world. Tony Blair is well liked by many and even his detractors can't argue with his disarming charm . . . all traits of your standard Ringo.

Colin Powell

At first glance, Colin Powell may seem like a typical George. He's thoughtful, not overly aggressive, and somewhat soft-spoken for someone in his position. However, Colin Powell is actually a Ringo. How can this be? One dominant trait of Ringos is that a great deal of their success comes from luck or just being in the right place at the right time. Former secretary Powell infamously benefited from just being there, too. He never voiced contradictory opinions too loudly and eventually made his way up the chain of command. Like other Ringos, he was just "happy to be here."

Boris Yeltsin

Dancin' Boris Yeltsin was another quintessential Ringo. His achievements were often overshadowed by his alcoholism and other personal failings. However, he put his mark on the Russian presidency and brought the country out of Communism and successfully into the eighteenth century.

Art, Music, Theater, Film, and Literature

Mick Jagger and Keith Richards

Like Bonny and Clyde or Antony and Cleopatra, the names Mick and Keith just go together. The Rolling Stones have a musical legacy equaled only by the Beatles, and it's all thanks to Mick Jagger and Keith Richards. While a little unusual for a leader, Mick is in fact a Ringo with a Paul minor. Mick doesn't take himself or his singing ability too seriously. Keith, a George, is more musically talented and helps to keep Mick's feet firmly planted on the ground.

Vincent Van Gogh

By many accounts, Vincent Van Gogh was as crazy as a loon, even if he didn't really cut off his own ear. He was truly an insane, artistic genius, putting him firmly in the John category. And, like many Johns, he died too early and underappreciated.

Jackson Pollock

Jackson Pollock is another quintessential John artist. He was a deeply troubled, alcoholic painter who despised the elitist art establishment in New York (turns out he loved Thomas Kinkade paintings). Amazingly, this John chose wisely in a spouse who supported and challenged him. Unfortunately, he was too much for Lee Krasner to control.

Salvador Dali

Many find it unbelievable that Salvador Dali, with his outrageous antics and wild public persona, was in fact a George. Beneath the twisted mustache was a man who cared deeply about only one thing, himself. Upon the outbreak of the Spanish Civil War, Dali fled the country, unwilling to take sides. After he returned to Spain, he made a number of pro-Franco statements. Many believe Dali wasn't a fascist, but simply would align himself with whomever was in power. This "cover your ass" trait is very common to Georges.

Rick James

Surprisingly, Rick James was a Paul both on and off stage. First, Rick, or "Mr. James" as we refer to him, took his music and image way too seriously. Let's face it, "Super Freak" isn't exactly Beethoven's Ninth. And those clothes? They make M. C. Hammer blush. In his love life, Rick wanted to be adored and in control—so much in control that he let his fists do the talking.

William Shakespeare

There is great conjecture by historians regarding Shakespeare. Many believe he was occasionally an Epstein and occasionally straight. Some believe he wrote all of his plays, while others felt it was a collaborative effort. Regardless of the full truth, Shakespeare was most definitely a George. First, Georges are often attracted to writing and to writing plays and to making money writing plays, preferring to be behind the curtain than in front. Second, in order to write his histories, Shakespeare had to be highly intellectual and well read—all traits common to Georges.

Stephen Ambrose

Ambrose truly had a gift for writing "popular" histories of such important figures as Eisenhower and Lewis and Clark. He also had a nasty little habit of occasionally plagiarizing. Like many Pauls in Beatleology, Ambrose was defensive about the charges to the point of being hostile. Like many Pauls, when backed into a corner, Ambrose made no excuses for his behavior.

George Orwell

Orwell is yet another George with a George Inner Beatle (along with George Washington, Curious George, and Boy George). This author's work explores life, politics, and the nature of government. His thoughtful analysis makes him clearly a George.

Andy Warhol

Most Georges hate pretension and the "in" crowd. Andy Warhol, however, relished it. At the time, many felt his works were in fact a hoax or put-on, which they may well have been. Either way, Andy challenged the collective concept of art and pushed it to new boundaries.

Charlton Heston

Charlton Heston is easily identifiable as a Paul. He possessed a strong, domineering personality. Heston was the ultimate movie star; he was tall, good looking, and full of charisma. Like other Pauls, there is no arguing that he ever doubted his own beliefs and talents. As a Paul, Heston could make brilliant decisions like publicly backing the civil rights movement. He could also make pig-headed decisions like speaking at an NRA event days after the Columbine shooting.

Bob Dylan

Bob Dylan is a classic John. He not only introduced the real John Lennon to marijuana, but inspired John's approach to music. Both men were dark, brooding, insecure, and highly talented composers. Like Lennon, Dylan's music defined a generation (a description both men despised). Dylan also hated the press and the asinine questions often asked of him and his music.

Sean Penn

Many Johns are drawn to acting and performing. This is often symptomatic of their psychological need to prove themselves. Sean Penn is no exception. While this talented actor has little left to prove, he definitely approaches his work with a chip on his shoulder. Similar to other Johns, Penn is extremely close to his family, but wary of outsiders like the press.

Jim Henson

This may come as a shock, but the creator of Kermit the Frog, *Sesame Street*, and the Muppets was a John. Only an artistic genius like Jim Henson could have come up with all those wonderful characters that were wholesome and at the same time slightly subversive.

Bill Cosby

The king of Jell-O Pudding Pops and family-friendly comedy is, surprisingly, a John. Cosby has a dark side and a real chip on his shoulder. Many African Americans are upset over his criticism of their community. This only makes Cosby more resolute in his convictions. Also like a typical John, Cosby has a profound sense of humor. Even though many see him as America's dad, we often forget he was a successful stand-up comedian.

Edward Norton

Hollywood actors who are thoughtful, well read, and pick challenging projects are hard to come by. Ed Norton is a rare exception. His Inner George has helped him play roles in films such as *Fight Club, The Painted Veil,* and *American History X.*

Andy Kaufman

Andy Kaufman's sense of humor, and his sense of the absurd, coupled with the fact that he was more than a little crazy, made him a John. Johns enjoy humor and challenging people with intellectual put-ons, like Kaufman's "impersonations" and wrestling. Like many Johns, Andy was far ahead of his time and many people simply weren't ready for him.

Paris Hilton

Sometimes you can have too much of a Ringo. Sure they're fun, easygoing, and love a good time, but that often becomes too much to take. Paris Hilton, like other Ringos, doesn't have a lot of talent. And sometimes her egotistical, hedonistic ways and ability to mock regular people make you start to realize why the terrorists hate our freedom.

Will Smith

The Fresh Prince of Bel Air is most definitely a Ringo. While Smith's actual talent is arguable, he is full of charm, good looks, and charisma. He's also disarming in a way only a Ringo can be. This Ringo definitely gets by on his personality.

Tommy Lee

Not surprisingly, many drummers are Ringos. Tommy Lee is no exception. Like Ringo, much of Tommy Lee's talent lies with his image and the size of his Johnson (and nowhere else). In keeping with his sign's personality traits, Tommy decided to marry a woman for her looks rather than her ability to fulfill him spiritually.

Sports

Muhammad Ali

Muhammad Ali (or Cassius Clay to his mother) felt he was the greatest of all time, an attribute common to Pauls. Ali knew how to put on a show that extended far beyond the boxing ring. He also had an innate ability when it came to self promotion just like all good Pauls.

Wilt Chamberlain

Wilt Chamberlain was arguably the best basketball player to ever live and a quintessential John. He was talented but also deeply troubled. He was often booed in games and seen as a distant, egotistical figure. Chamberlain also loved women and sex, as described in his notorious autobiography.

Joe DiMaggio

Joe DiMaggio was a complicated figure. On one hand, he was a gifted athlete and highly philanthropic, often giving to children's charities. On the other hand, Joltin' Joe could be a joltin' jerk. He was conceited and self-indulgent. Joe even considered suing Simon and Garfunkel over a lyric to their song, "Mrs. Robinson." Taken together, those two aspects of his personality definitely make him a John.

Kobe Bryant

Kobe Bryant is a classic sports John. He's harbored some animosity most of his career. First, while he is an African American, he didn't grow up in that community, but lived much of his youth abroad. Due to this, some have said he's not truly "black." Kobe has spent a great deal of his career proving himself and not necessarily making friends along the way. He's also notoriously arrogant.

Barry Bonds

The record for most home runs is held by a George. Barry Bonds exhibits many George characteristics. First, he's a highly private man. He's soft-spoken and dislikes interviews and the media in general (well, who doesn't?). And like Georges, he is very talented at what he does: ~~take steroids~~ hit the baseball into the stands.

Tom Brady

A good-looking quarterback like Tom Brady could only be a Paul. He's popular with sports fans and the ladies alike. While he's considered a nice guy (he won "Sportsman of the Year"), he still has that drive to compete and win only found in a Paul.

Yogi Berra

When looking at Yogi Berra's life as a whole, it's easy to see that he is clearly a Ringo. Sure he has said plenty of cute, endearing one-liners, as Ringos are prone to do. But his athletic accomplishments are underappreciated. People often forget that this Ringo was a three-time league MVP and fifteen-time All Star player. They just remember his wit and ability to mangle the English language (a trait Ringo Starr had in spades; Ringo Starr: "Eight days a week." Yogi Berra: "It's like déjà vu all over again.").

Magic Johnson

As an outspoken member of the "show time" Lakers, Earvin "Magic" Johnson is clearly a Paul. He's highly popular, outgoing, and *loves* to be in charge on and off the court. Magic was a dynamic leader on the Lakers squad for a number of years. He received the MVP three times during his career. His Magic Johnson Enterprises is now an economic force in the Los Angeles area. Only a Paul could achieve all of that.

LeBron James

No doubt about it, "King James" of the Cleveland Cavaliers is a Paul. His skill at basketball is only matched by his skill at self-promotion and trying to earn a buck. He's stated he wants to be the first billionaire athlete. While he often comes off as fun and approachable in commercials and *Saturday Night Live* appearances, LeBron is highly driven to win and, more important, earn money. All of these traits put him squarely in the Paul category.

Lance Armstrong

Lance Armstrong is most definitely a Paul. Only a Paul could take sole credit for winning all of those Tour de France championships when cycling is truly a team sport. And only a Paul could still claim to be a winner when the amount of illegal substances he ingested makes Lou Reed look like Mother Teresa.

Larry Bird

Like many Ringos, Larry Bird had gritty working-class roots before being projected into basketball superstardom. Larry was a notoriously hard worker on and off the court. And, like other Ringos, he was highly respected and liked by everyone who came into contact with him.

Joe Montana

As one of the most successful quarterbacks in football, it might be hard to believe Joe Montana is a George. Usually it takes a Paul or John Inner Beatle to win four Super Bowls. But Joe has a deeper, more thoughtful side. Now in retirement, Joe enjoys being an equestrian and making wine.

Chapter 13

IN CLOSING —
ALL TOGETHER NOW

Now that you have made a breakthrough to Beatleology and have used it to discover yourself and improve your life, as well as the lives of those around you, it is time to put the pieces together.

Come to Terms with Your Sign

Each individual must come to accept themselves as the Beatle Sign they are, secure in the knowledge that they are all equally important. Even if you fancied yourself a John but are in fact a Paul, it's nothing to be ashamed of. We have to embrace who we are. Accepting yourself and your sign is key to contentment.

Learn the Beatle Sign of Those Around You

In order to understand your fellow humans, it is critical to learn to recognize the Beatle Sign of others. Discovering the signs of your family, coworkers, and friends is fundamental to positive relationships. Utilize the quiz in Chapter 2 and the descriptions of each sign to recognize the other Beatles in your life. Only then can the Beatleologist progress to the next level.

Embrace Your Fellow Beatles

The third step involves welcoming all of the Beatle Signs into your life. If your husband is a Ringo, learn to live with his lack of seriousness. If your father is a John, you need to accept his quirks. If we can learn to harness the positive qualities of each sign, our lives will be happier and more productive. For instance, you can use a Paul's perfectionism to your advantage at home and in the workplace. Aligning with a Ringo can make you more popular.

Come Together

Last, all Beatle Signs must learn to come together (right now) to work harmoniously in romance, work, and family. We need to recognize we can't do it all alone. Life requires that we get a long with others. How we accomplish that is up to us. By putting our knowledge of Beatleology into practice, we can begin to find balance in life.

Beatleologists in Harmony

The Alpha Beatles' musical careers can be divided into three parts. The early years of the band, the later years, and the individual members' solo years. Each phase has something to tell us about Beatleologists working together.

The Early Years

The band the Beatles came together one by one and not until the final addition of Ringo did it achieve true harmony. In the early Quarrymen days, before John invited Paul into the band, there was simply too much John. There was brilliance but also flippancy and laziness; a sense that every bad poem and naughty cartoon he produced was sheer genius. It took the filtering, refining influence, and work ethic of Paul to shape it into something more coherent. This partnership was the basis of many of the most loved songs of all times. This was a good start, but these two very powerful signs badly needed a more moderating influence. This influence came in the form of Alpha George. George Harrison, a true virtuoso on the guitar, was able to take the outpouring of creativity from John and Paul and apply his more quiet and thoughtful talent to communicate it to an audience. Like many gifted people, John, Paul, and George had very strong personalities and were not always easy to get along with. Internal strife threatened to derail the band just as it was on the brink of success. Enter Ringo Starr. In addition to providing the rock-solid drumbeat the band needed to showcase their talents, Alpha Ringo was the social rock on which the band could depend to keep their sometimes erratic personalities grounded. Having been invited into the band just as their first hit was to be released, Ringo always felt a genuine sense of good fortune and took the most satisfaction from the band's success. Had this joyousness not rubbed off on the rest of the band, they might not have lasted as long as they did and humanity would have been robbed of its greatest social and artistic phenomenon. Only with all four parts of the cosmic quartet assembled could the Beatles accomplish everything they did. Together they not only wrote the soundtrack of a generation, they transformed world culture, spirituality, and political thought.

Later Years

In the later years, personality conflicts, destructive romantic relationships, and multiple fiascos with their business dealings started to slowly erode the group's cohesion. Slowly but surely, this led the band to their breakup in 1970. Many individual factors fanned the fire of discontent that spelled the end of the Beatles. Paradoxically, two of the main factors were not enough time in each other's company *and* too much togetherness. When the band was touring "eight days a week" they were constantly together, trapped in hotels besieged by adoring fans. Because of this forced confinement and the necessity of teamwork on a grueling tour schedule, they had no choice but to keep their divergent Beatle Signs in check and work together. After the band quit touring in 1966, those strong personalities were able to take control of the egos and made collaboration more difficult. Conversely, the group never took a significant break from the various duties of the band, causing burnout that hastened their breakup. If they had taken, say, a year off as many bands do today, they might have stayed together longer.

With success comes the ability to play by one's own rules. This only led to more conflict; John Lennon is probably the most dramatic example. With the help of Yoko Ono and his increasing dependency on drugs, Alpha John's Beatle Sign tendency to think everything he did was deep and significant grew unchecked. The fact that the Fab Four as a group had succeeded beyond his wildest dreams didn't prevent John from the idea that they were out to get him and hold him back artistically.

Pauls are bossy and like things done their own way. As John withdrew as leader of the band, Alpha Paul bullied his way into the position. This caused much resentment from John Lennon and George Harrison.

Alpha George, always a talented musician, had progressed as an artist and songwriter and desired more creative control and album space for his compositions. With his George-like tendency toward quiet passive-aggression, Alpha George was unable to successfully fight for his agenda and ultimately found it easier to withdraw from the band.

Only Ringo is blameless. Always the affable down-to-earth one, he remained true to his Beatle Sign and was too smart to let petty bickering get in the way of a good thing. Finally these alienating influences, along with the death of Brian Epstein, and several failed business ventures by Apple Corps, spelled the end. Their relatively short existence is not necessarily a bad thing. By quitting after *Let It Be*, they went out on top. Had the band continued for many years, it might well have suffered the fate of many bands that stay together forever. They might have had their music stagnate and become predictable or fall victim to modern celebrity pop culture. It was much better to have the group disband than to see the Fab Four kowtow to Donald Trump on *The Celebrity Apprentice*. The flame that burns twice as bright burns half as long.

Solo Years

All four Beatles went on to successful solo careers. However, because each one is only one-quarter of the cosmic quartet, they were unable to achieve the brilliance of the group. Without their band mates, the music of each Alpha Beatle reflected each individual's Beatle Sign exclusively and suffered from a lack of the balance provided by the other three.

In his solo career, John was free to become more political with a large focus on ending the Vietnam War. His music and performance art with Yoko also became more experimental, psychedelic, and in some cases flippant. Beatle Sign Johns tend to be their own worst enemies (i.e., "more popular than Jesus"), and in many cases John Lennon's sense of the absurd was counterproductive to his legitimate work for peace and political reform.

Beatle Sign Pauls love the spotlight and being in charge. Paul McCartney pursued the most mainstream and financially successful solo career of any of the group. Always a talented songwriter and charismatic performer, Paul's post-Beatle career lacked the progressive edginess that John and George brought to the table. With that absence of his band mates, Paul's "cute one" characteristics made his solo career wildly successful but lacking in artistic merit.

In the band's later years, George Harrison felt creatively stifled by the powerhouse of Lennon-McCartney songwriting and Paul's ultimate domination of the band. Georges work well in groups and George Harrison teamed up with many other talented musicians such as Eric Clapton, Bob Dylan, and the Traveling Wilburys to produce a lot of good music. True to his Beatle Sign nature as "the shy one," George had trouble seizing the spotlight to become a huge star. However, as a George, that's probably how he wanted it.

As Ringo Starr said, "I'm rich and famous and adored by millions. Let's stick with that." True to his Beatle Sign nature, Ringo Starr has probably enjoyed himself the most in his solo work. Always the friendly, lovable, nonthreatening "funny one," Ringo has had tremendous fun with many different projects, including acting and playing with his friends in the All Starr Band. Ringos have a tendency to not get proper credit for their talents. Without his more high-profile Beatle mates, Ringo has failed to achieve the notoriety in his post-band work that he deserves. He is the only Beatle not to be in the Rock and Roll Hall of Fame for his solo career, but he is too busy enjoying life to care.

Conclusion

The experiences of the Alpha Beatles in their early, later, and solo years have much to teach Beatleologists about life and the nature of the cosmos.

The early years of the band were truly a golden age. The four Beatle Sign quarters came together in perfect balance with incredible results that vastly improved the world as we know it. Beatleologists should take the lessons of the early years to heart and know that even though there is friction with your fellow band mates, you should be proud to play your role in the group. Only together can there be perfect harmony.

The later years of the band teach us that being too strong in our individual Beatle Signs can still produce incredible results but rarely lead to harmony. Beatleologists need to be wary of the trap of thinking that their sign is the best and that they should dominate others. If the world were willing to work together as a whole instead of feuding as separate nations, ethnic groups, and religions, it would be a much better place.

The solo years show us the individual strengths of the four Beatle Signs. Each Alpha Beatle went on to accomplish much after the band's breakup. However, the question must be asked, how much success would they have achieved without the notoriety of the band? Would any of them have made it on their own? The lesson for Beatleologists is that your individual sign is great and you can do many things, but without teamwork and the input of your band mates, life is more difficult and lonely.

In Closing

Once again, congratulations on taking the next step in your personal development and in the evolution of mankind! You've learned much about yourself, others, the world around you, and how it all comes back to the unifying theme of existence: the Beatles. But the journey has just begun. There are still hundreds of people in the world ignorant of the principles of Beatleology and therefore incapable of achieving true harmony with existence. It is your mission to bring the truth to those people. In this quest, always remember that whether you are a John, Paul, George, or Ringo, we are all cosmic band mates playing one big gig in the cosmic Cavern Club of the Beatle-verse.

APPENDIX

I Am the Walrus Quiz—Answer Key

Here is the answer key to the I Am the Walrus Quiz from Chapter 2. Scoring is easy: Simply, check your answers for every question and tally each John, Paul, George, and Ringo you scored. The most frequent Beatle you tallied corresponds to your Beatle Sign. If you have vastly more answers of one letter than the rest, you are closer to a "true," or "pure" sign. Your second-highest score (if there is a clear second) corresponds to your minor sign (see Chapter 7).

Caution! We suggest that you remain seated when tabulating the questions. Often, the life-changing epiphany that can occur is too much for the human mind to handle. Results ranging from fainting to crazed hysteria have been reported.

Answer Key

Part I: Work

1. Ⓐ John Ⓑ Ringo Ⓒ George Ⓓ Paul

2. Ⓐ George Ⓑ Paul Ⓒ Ringo Ⓓ John

3. Ⓐ Paul Ⓑ John Ⓒ Ringo Ⓓ George

4. Ⓐ George Ⓑ Ringo Ⓒ Paul D – John

5. Ⓐ Ringo Ⓑ John Ⓒ George Ⓓ Paul

6. Ⓐ George Ⓑ Paul Ⓒ John Ⓓ Ringo

7. Ⓐ Paul Ⓑ John Ⓒ Ringo Ⓓ George

8. Ⓐ John Ⓑ George Ⓒ Paul Ⓓ Ringo

9. Ⓐ Ringo Ⓑ Paul Ⓒ John Ⓓ George

10. Ⓐ George Ⓑ Ringo Ⓒ John Ⓓ Paul

Part II: Relationships

1. Ⓐ Paul Ⓑ John Ⓒ George Ⓓ Ringo

2. Ⓐ Ringo Ⓑ George Ⓒ Paul Ⓓ John

3. Ⓐ John Ⓑ George Ⓒ Ringo Ⓓ Paul

4. Ⓐ George Ⓑ Paul Ⓒ John Ⓓ Ringo

5. Ⓐ Paul Ⓑ John Ⓒ George Ⓓ Ringo

6. Ⓐ John Ⓑ Paul Ⓒ Ringo Ⓓ George

7. Ⓐ Ringo Ⓑ Paul Ⓒ John Ⓓ George

8. Ⓐ George Ⓑ John Ⓒ Paul Ⓓ Ringo

9. Ⓐ Paul Ⓑ George Ⓒ John Ⓓ Ringo

10. Ⓐ John Ⓑ Ringo Ⓒ George Ⓓ Paul

Part III: Family

1. Ⓐ John Ⓑ Ringo Ⓒ George Ⓓ Paul

2. Ⓐ Ringo Ⓑ George Ⓒ Paul Ⓓ John

3. Ⓐ George Ⓑ Paul Ⓒ Ringo Ⓓ John

4. Ⓐ Paul Ⓑ John Ⓒ George Ⓓ Ringo

5. Ⓐ John Ⓑ Ringo Ⓒ Paul Ⓓ George

Part IV: Morality

1. Ⓐ Paul Ⓑ George Ⓒ John Ⓓ Ringo

2. Ⓐ Paul Ⓑ Ringo Ⓒ George Ⓓ John

3. Ⓐ George Ⓑ Paul Ⓒ John Ⓓ Ringo

4. Ⓐ John Ⓑ Ringo Ⓒ George Ⓓ Paul

5. Ⓐ Ringo Ⓑ Paul Ⓒ John Ⓓ George

Part V: Religion and Spirituality

1. Ⓐ Paul Ⓑ George Ⓒ Ringo Ⓓ John

2. Ⓐ Ringo Ⓑ John Ⓒ George Ⓓ Paul

3. Ⓐ George Ⓑ Paul Ⓒ Ringo Ⓓ John

4. Ⓐ John Ⓑ Ringo Ⓒ Paul Ⓓ George

5. Ⓐ John Ⓑ George Ⓒ Paul Ⓓ Ringo

Part VI: Money

1. Ⓐ John Ⓑ George Ⓒ Ringo Ⓓ Paul

2. Ⓐ Ringo Ⓑ John Ⓒ George Ⓓ Paul

3. Ⓐ Paul Ⓑ John Ⓒ George Ⓓ Ringo

4. Ⓐ John Ⓑ George Ⓒ Paul Ⓓ Ringo

5. Ⓐ Ringo Ⓑ Paul Ⓒ George Ⓓ John

Part VII: Miscellaneous

1. Ⓐ John Ⓑ Paul Ⓒ George Ⓓ Ringo

2. Ⓐ George Ⓑ Ringo Ⓒ John Ⓓ Paul

3. Ⓐ Paul Ⓑ Ringo Ⓒ George Ⓓ John

4. Ⓐ John Ⓑ Paul Ⓒ Ringo Ⓓ George

5. Ⓐ Paul Ⓑ George Ⓒ Ringo Ⓓ John

INDEX

Index

ABOUT THE AUTHORS

Brothers Adam and Roger Jaquette were born in the Seattle area and grew up listening to Beatles music, thanks to their baby boomer parents. As kids, they remember singing along to "With a Little Help from My Friends."

Roger earned a BA in drama from the University of Washington, where he wrote and produced numerous plays. He later pursued graduate studies in film and television production.

Adam holds a BFA from New York University and an MFA from Chapman University in dramatic writing. He has written numerous screenplays, which have been optioned by the Motion Picture Corporation of America (*Dumb & Dumber, Kingpin*) and was a finalist in the Scriptapalooza screenwriting contest. His articles for children have also been published in *Skipping Stones Magazine*. He currently teaches elementary school.

Adam and Roger currently reside in Southern California and are still listening to the music of the Fab Four.